Social Issues
in Literature

Issues of Class
in Jane Austen's
Pride and Prejudice

Other Books in the Social Issues in Literature Series:

Social Issues
in Literature

Issues of Class
in Jane Austen's
Pride and Prejudice

Claudia Durst Johnson, Book Editor

GREENHAVEN PRESS
A part of Gale, Cengage Learning

GALE
CENGAGE Learning™

Detroit • New York • San Francisco • New Haven, Conn • Waterville, Maine • London

GALE
CENGAGE Learning

Christine Nasso, *Publisher*
Elizabeth Des Chenes, *Managing Editor*

© 2009 Greenhaven Press, a part of Gale, Cengage Learning

Gale and Greenhaven Press are registered trademarks used herein under license.

For more information, contact:
Greenhaven Press
27500 Drake Rd.
Farmington Hills, MI 48331-3535
Or you can visit our Internet site at gale.cengage.com

For product information and technology assistance, contact us at

Gale Customer Support, 1-800-877-4253
For permission to use material from this text or product, submit all requests online at www.cengage.com/permissions

Further permissions questions can be emailed to permissionrequest@cengage.com

Articles in Greenhaven Press anthologies are often edited for length to meet page requirements. In addition, original titles of these works are changed to clearly present the main thesis and to explicitly indicate the author's opinion. Every effort is made to ensure that Greenhaven Press accurately reflects the original intent of the authors. Every effort has been made to trace the owners of copyrighted material.

Cover photograph reproduced by permission of © Pictorial Press Ltd/Alamy.

LIBRARY OF CONGRESS CATALOGING-IN-PUBLICATION DATA

Issues of class in Jane Austen's Pride and prejudice / Claudia Durst Johnson, book editor.
    p. cm. -- (Social issues in literature)
Includes bibliographical references and index.
ISBN-13: 978-0-7377-4258-9 (hbk.)
ISBN-13: 978-0-7377-4259-6 (pbk.)
  1. Austen, Jane, 1775-1817. Pride and prejudice. 2. Social classes in literature.
I. Johnson, Claudia D.
  PR4034.P72I77 2008
  823'.7--dc22
                                                        2008021484

Printed in the United States of America
1 2 3 4 5 6 7 12 11 10 09 08

Contents

Introduction

Published in 1813 and set in the late eighteenth century, Jane Austen's *Pride and Prejudice* is a record of upper- and middle-class English society in a time of colossal social change, created by the Industrial Revolution and affected by the upheaval caused by the French Revolution.

The social pyramid in England in Austen's day was intricate and in flux:

- At the top were royalty and nobility, numbering about 3,000 people.
- Beneath them in rank were 50,000 upper-class titled aristocrats.
- Then came 40,000 upper-class clergy, merchants, bankers, upper civil servants, and lawyers.
- Beneath this rank was the upper middle-class, constituting 150,000 independent gentry, 20,000 professionals, 70,000 military officers, and 75,000 lesser clergy. This was the world of *Pride and Prejudice*.
- The majority of the population, some 15 million people, was made up of the lower and working classes of small businessmen, artisans, farm workers, servants, soldiers and sailors, and paupers. These lower classes are largely invisible in *Pride and Prejudice*.

Austen's focus is on the aristocracy, the landed and unlanded gentry, the professionals, and the officers.

The Industrial Revolution was creating rapid social change in the eighteenth century. The divisions between classes were less rigid. A titled person's marriage to an untitled person had earlier been unheard of. Even in the late eighteenth century, the courtship of Austen, the daughter of a poor clergyman, with an upper-class young man was ended when his family sent him away because of the difference in their rank and her poverty. But as industry grew and middle-class men were able to amass fortunes as industrialists, upward social mobility grew, as did social interaction and marriages between those who had inherited rank and those who had achieved it.

Austen and her heroine, Elizabeth Bennet, lived in small, sleepy agricultural towns. Bath, the nearest town of consequence, where Austen lived for a time, had been the primary playground for the upper classes from about the 1740s onward. The warm Roman baths, for which the town was named, were its initial tourist attractions, and the town, which existed for the wealthy, included theaters, fashionable ballrooms, and gambling halls. Bath was also notable as a place where matchmaking occurred, as wealthy singles without impressive rank from birth looked for mates with greater social standing, and members of the upper classes, without money, looked for wealthy partners. Austen satirizes Bath society in *Northanger Abbey* (1817). The social life of Bath was repeated on a smaller scale in the villages throughout the area.

Class distinctions are intrinsic to *Pride and Prejudice*. Mr. Bennet, father of five girls, is a "gentleman" with enough money to keep a house, hire servants, and maintain horses. But because he has no sons, at his death his inheritance and house will go to his nearest male relative, leaving any unmarried daughter with nowhere to live and an insufficient income from their mother.

Darcy benefits from both inherited rank and wealth. Bingley seems to have achieved his position in society through a family of industrialists who accrued wealth. He illustrates the loosening of strict class boundaries.

Collins is a middle-class clergyman, living in a small village, respectable enough to find support and hospitality from one of the true aristocrats in the novel, Lady Catherine de

Bourgh. Lady Catherine offers an unflattering portrait of upper-class snobbery. She is an egotistical bully, and Collins is her silly sycophant.

The Gardiners, Elizabeth's aunt and uncle, are well-bred, successful tradespeople who are, nevertheless, scorned and snubbed by members of the upper class because they live in an undesirable commercial London neighborhood adjoining their business.

The officers, young and old, in a militia formed to protect the English homeland were also classified as "gentlemen" but were socially inferior to regular army and navy officers and to landed gentry, unless their families and connections were in the upper class. Wickham, the darling of the militia as well as the ladies of the village, has the appearance and manners of a nobly born young man, but he is actually the son of a care-taker of an estate. With the sponsorship of his father's noble employer, Wickham eventually secures an officer's commission in the military, but he remains the scoundrel of the novel.

The following articles discuss various aspects in the novel of the upper and middle classes in England shortly after a revolution in France that threatened the very foundations of the class system. The articles also study the divisions of rank even within social groups and families, based primarily on gender, education, wealth, appearance, intelligence, and socia-bility. Females occupied a lower rank than males in society and in their own families, as can be seen in the entailment that left the Bennet daughters out of an inheritance. Educa-tion, often provided by a wealthier sponsor, was a key to a more respectable social position, as can be seen in the case of Mr. Collins. Wealth, especially during and after the Industrial Revolution, was a way to buy rank; this was likely the case with Bingley. Beautiful women, like Jane and Elizabeth, were more highly ranked than homely women, and Wickham ini-tially gains his position in local society because of his looks.

The articles with which this volume closes examine issues of class and a woman's place in current society.

Chronology

1775

Jane Austen is born on December 16 in Steventon, Hampshire, the daughter of a clergyman.

1785–1786

Austen and her sister, Cassandra, attend Abbey boarding school in Reading.

1782–1784

Austen writes fiction and plays for the family.

1787–1793

Austen writes her Juvenilia, a three-volume collection of parodies intended for the amusement of her family.

circa 1795

Austen begins writing "Elinor and Marianne," an early version of *Sense and Sensibility.*

1796–1797

Austen writes "First Impressions," an early version of *Pride and Prejudice.* Attempts to publish it fail.

1798–1799

Austen writes early drafts of *Northanger Abbey*, originally called "Susan" and later "Catherine."

1801–1802

The Austens move to the city of Bath.

1805

Austen's father dies.

1809

After moving around from place to place in Bath and Southampton, Austen, Cassandra, and their mother are provided with comfortable quarters in a house on the estate of Austen's brother Edward.

1811

Austen publishes *Sense and Sensibility*.

1813

Pride and Prejudice is published.

1814

Mansfield Park is published.

1815

Emma is published.

1817

A third edition of *Pride and Prejudice* is published. After a yearlong illness, Austen dies on July 18 in Winchester, where she is buried in the cathedral. *Northanger Abbey* and *Persuasion* are published posthumously.

Social Issues in Literature

CHAPTER 1

Background on Jane Austen

Rural Gentry

Gary Kelly

Gary Kelly, holder of the Canada Research Chair in Language at the University of Alberta, is the author of Revolutionary Feminism: The Mind and Career of Mary Wollstonecraft *(1992) and* Women, Writing, and Revolution, 1790–1827 *(1993).*

The portrayal of the eighteenth-century class system, which is so prominent in Jane Austen's work, is a reflection of her own family and surroundings. Her father was born into a family of tradesmen but received an Oxford education with the help of wealthier friends and relatives and became a professional—a clergyman. Her mother, of a somewhat higher rank, raised the social standing of the family so they could mingle and marry with the gentry, even some of whom held titles. Austen and her family read many of the popular novels of the day, written by and for the professional middle class, which denounced and satirized the aristocracy and members of the middle class who imitated upper-class fashion. Against the background of the French Revolution and the controversy it provoked in England, novelists and social philosophers also expressed fear that the lower classes would rise up.

Jane Austen was born into the rural professional middle class. Her father, George Austen (1731–1805), was a country clergyman at Steventon, a small village in the southern English county of Hampshire. He had risen by merit from a Kentish family in trade and the lower professions. Jane Austen's mother, Cassandra Leigh Austen (1739–1827), was from a higher social rank, minor gentry related distantly to titled people, but once she married the Reverend Austen in 1764 she entered wholeheartedly and with humor into the domestic life and responsibilities of managing a household economy by no means luxurious, bearing eight children—six sons and two daughters. In this setting the Austens mingled easily with other gentrified professionals and with local gentry families.

Yet they were also linked, though tenuously in some ways, with the larger world of fashionable society and of patronage, politics, and state. George Austen owed his education at Oxford University to his own merit as a student at Tonbridge School, but he owed his clerical position, or "living," at Steventon to the patronage of a wealthy relative, Thomas Knight of Godmersham Park, Kent, who held the appointment in his gift. Later the Knights, who were childless, adopted one of the Austens' sons, Edward, as their own son and heir to their estates in Kent and Hampshire. One of Jane Austen's cousins, Elizabeth (Eliza) Hancock, married a French aristocrat—Jean Capotte, Comte de Feuillide. The comte was guillotined during the French Revolution, and Eliza later married Jane Austen's brother Henry. Local friends of the Austens included the Reverend George Lefroy and his wife, Anne, sister of an eccentric, novel-writing, obsessively aristocratic Kentish squire, Sir Samuel Egerton Brydges. "Madam Lefroy," as she was known locally, was lively and energetic, wrote verses (some of which got published), enthusiastically embraced the contemporary literature and culture of Sensibility, and engaged in fashionable philanthropy among the local poor. . . .

Rising in Rank and Fortune

Austen's brothers, apart from Edward, went in for genteel but demanding professions. Her eldest brother, James (1765–1819), who had literary tastes and intellectual interests, followed his father's path to St. John's College, Oxford, and eventually became his father's successor as rector of Steventon. Her second brother, George (1766–1838), was born handicapped and did not play a part in the family life. The third son was Edward

(1767–1852), who was adopted by the Knights and took over the Knight estates in 1797. The fourth child, Henry (1771–1850), was the liveliest, the most adventurous and the most speculative of the Austens. Like James, he went to St. John's College, Oxford, but instead of taking orders upon graduation he joined the army, gave that up for the relatively ungenteel line of banking, and married his glamorous widowed cousin, Eliza de Feuillide. When his bank failed in 1816 during the economic crisis following the Napoleonic Wars, he fell back on his father's profession and became a clergyman. The next child, Cassandra (1773–1845), was Jane's closest friend throughout her life and was known in the family for her steady character and sound judgment. Like Jane, she never married. Her fiancé, the Reverend Thomas Fowle, died while serving as a military chaplain in the West Indies in 1797. The two youngest Austen boys, Francis (1774–1865) and Charles (1779–1852), were trained at the Royal Naval Academy at Portsmouth, became officers, served in the French wars, and rose to the rank of admiral.

Family and the World

Though the issues and interests of the wider world may have come from afar somewhat muffled, they did flow through the rectory at Steventon, and later—less muffled—through the other habitations and homes of Jane Austen as well. But the rectory at Steventon with its lively, frank, and intimate yet open family life was her first and formative home. Her parents had a close and happy marriage. Her mother was thoroughly domestic yet commonsensical and humorous; her father was kind, loving, and encouraging to his daughters as well as his sons. Jane, known as "Jenny" in the family, was well liked by her brothers, who were often at home even while students at Oxford or Portsmouth, and who visited their sisters when they were away briefly at school. . . .

Class and Fiction

Austen's main interest, however, was in the varieties of prose fiction. For example "Frederic and Elfrida: A Novel" burlesques the contemporary sentimental novel, with its ideal hero and heroine, interspersed letters and verses, elegant dialogue, noble feelings, pathetic incidents, and plot of delayed courtship. "Jack and Alice: A Novel," "Edgar and Emma: A Tale," "Henry and Eliza: A Novel," and "The Beautiful Cassandra: A Novel in Twelve Chapters" burlesque such novel conventions as the opening in medias res, the use of short racy chapters, names taken from *Burke's Peerage*, scenes of fashionable dissipation, extensive use of correspondence, inset narratives, fatal attractions, and glamorously distressed protagonists. "The Generous Curate: A Moral Tale," "The Adventures of Mr Harley," "Sir William Mountague," and "Memoirs of Mr Clifford" burlesque the newly popular form of the tale, or brief narrative, often packed with incident and characters lightly sketched, in contrast to the more extended treatment of "sentiment" in novels. The epistolary novel, still much in vogue and the most obviously "sentimental" form of fiction by the 1780s, is burlesqued in "Amelia Webster," "The Three Sisters: A Novel," "Love and Freindship [*sic*]: A Novel in a Series of Letters," and "Lesley Castle: An Unfinished Novel in Letters." The last two, along with "Evelyn" and "Catherine; or, The Bower," are more extended satires on novelistic "heroinism," and several of these burlesques suggest a connection between sentimentalism, which was a common object of criticism in the Austen family, and other kinds of social and even political transgression. A fragment of a burlesque apparently to be called "The Female Philosopher" indicates that Austen was familiar with the increasing tendency in the 1790s to associate Sentimentalism, female appropriation of "philosophy" or social criticism from the period before the French Revolution, and the feminism of writers such as Mary Wollstonecraft and Mary Hays, inspired by the egalitarian doctrines of the Revolution. . . .

Jane Austen, author of Pride and Prejudice, *is dressed in eighteenth-century fashion.* Public Domain.

Furthermore, critical response to classic and contemporary literature was no mere aesthetic diversion at that time, but a major way of participating in civic culture. "Literature of the day," as it was called, included novels, plays, light verse as well as more serious poetry, magazines, and so on; this literature expressed and reflected the interests and concerns of those who wrote and read it, and these writers and readers were, like the Austens, mainly professional middle-class people. They condemned what they saw as aristocratic snobbery, upper-class decadence, and the patronage system that spread from the royal court and government through the rest of society. They also condemned middle-class emulation of their social "betters" and upper-class cultural domination of society through the fashion system, or "the *ton*." During the 1780s and 1790s, for example, middle-class observers were repeatedly scandalized by the moral misconduct and abuse of social position by the Prince of Wales and his brothers, supposedly the leaders of society. At the same time, the middle classes were becoming increasingly concerned about the condition and the culture of the lower classes. Much middle-class social criticism warned against contamination from the "vulgar." Such warnings became more urgent during the "Revolution Debate" of the 1790s, when the middle and upper classes had to take sides on the nature and significance of the French Revolution for Britain.

At the same time, many social critics complained that "literature of the day" contributed to what it attacked—that it was part of the very "fashion system" it condemned. "Fashionable novels," "indecent plays," and "sentimental" writing of various kinds were condemned for spreading decadent upper-class values and practices to eager middle-class—and especially female—readers. The Austen family kept up with "literature of the day" and were aware of its important and controversial place in civic life. . . .

Education

The education of Austen and her sister was not nearly as thorough and systematic as that offered their brothers. While the men would have to prepare for a profession and therefore spend their formative years accumulating intellectual and moral capital for the future, the only career open to women of the Austens' class was that of wife and mother. The sisters were prepared accordingly with some training in "accomplishments," that is, "elegant" skills such as music, drawing, dancing, and comportment. Too close emotionally to be separated for schooling, despite their difference in age, the sisters were taken to study with Ann Cooper Cawley, the widow of a head of an Oxford college, in 1783. . . . In 1784 the sisters were sent to the Abbey School in Reading, where intellectual training was little emphasized. In December 1786 the girls returned home, where they received the majority of whatever education they ever had and largely educated themselves. . . .

The Novel and Social Comment

The Austens realized and appreciated the potential of the novel for social criticism and moral discourse at a time when most critics condemned novels as immoral, disseminators of decadent court culture, and subliterature fit only for women (though dangerously seductive for the supposedly weak female intellect and strong female imagination). . . .

Austen, Society, and Courtship

Until 1801 Austen lived in her family home at Steventon, reading the literature of the day, rereading her favorite authors, maintaining her local visiting network, discussing the characters and vicissitudes of new acquaintances and old friends, visiting her brother Edward and his family in Kent, dancing at balls given by the local gentry, accompanying her family to Bath for the recreations and social life of an elegant spa town, and keeping up with issues of the day, such as the long trial (1788–1794) in the House of Commons of Warren Hastings, first governor general of British India, on charges of corruption and abuse of office. . . .

In December 1795 she fell in love herself, with Thomas Langlois Lefroy, a graduate of Trinity College, Dublin, who was visiting his uncle and aunt. Recognizing that the young man would be disinherited if he married the daughter of a penniless clergyman, Madam Lefroy cut short the courtship by sending her nephew away. . . .

Class Satire

The novel was being used extensively in the Revolution debate of the 1790s: the struggle to lead the "political nation" and its immediate supporters and dependents (which could be equated with the reading public) into coalition either with politicized artisans and the lower-middle classes or with the landed gentry. In the late 1790s and early 1800s, however, writers turned to representing the reconciliation of social differences and conflicts that had threatened to take Britain, like France, over the brink of revolution in the early and mid 1790s and that continued to cause concern for the preservation of Britain's unity and empire against challenge from Napoleonic France. Women, conventionally seen as social mediators, were quick to take up the theme of national reconciliation in their writings, while avoiding overt discussion of the "unfeminine" subject of politics. Yet such writers wanted to continue the longstanding, middle-class critique of upper-class decadence, lower-class unreason, and middle-class social emulation of either.

Austen's novels participate in this post-Revolutionary literary movement. Austen began several novels in the latter half of the 1790s, though they were not published for some years, and then they were much altered. An epistolary novella, published after her death by her nephew as *Lady Susan*, in the second edition of his *Memoir of Jane Austen* (1871), depicts a selfish and witty courtly coquette. The text is partly a satirical exaggeration of the fashionable novels that portrayed such characters with apparent disapproval for fascinated and scandalized middle-class readers. . . .

Jane Austen: Class in Life and Work

John Lauber

John Lauber, professor emeritus of English at the University of Alberta, has published widely on Jane Austen and is the author of Sir Walter Scott *(1966).*

While most of her six brothers rose higher in social rank, professional importance, and wealth than their parents, Jane Austen and her only sister, Cassandra, were unable to rise in rank. Nor were they able to have the educations of their brothers. In families more comfortably situated than the Austens, the educating of daughters was enhanced by governesses, but the sum of Austen's and her sister's formal education was attendance at a boarding school for a couple years. Vocation was also affected by class and gender. The only fitting vocation for women of the middle and upper classes was marriage. But despite her vigorous efforts to secure a husband and two promising relationships, Austen never married. The fact that she had no fortune and was intelligent might have been offputting to other potential suitors. No female members of her class would have been allowed to work outside the home, married or not. So Austen's rank was an important factor in her taking up the vocation of writer after her brother Edward had rescued his mother and sisters from the poverty in which George Austen left them upon his death.

Jane Austen was born on 16 December 1775 in the village of Steventon in central England. Like the heroes, and also the fools, of several of her novels, her father, George Austen, was an Anglican clergyman, the rector of Steventon. Jane's mother, Cassandra, was a minister's daughter. It must have been a

John Lauber, *Jane Austen*. Belmont, CA: Twayne Publishers, 1993. Copyright © 1993 by Twayne Publishers. All rights reserved. Reproduced by permission of Gale, a part of Cengage Learning.

crowded household, with two daughters and five [sons] (besides a sixth, apparently retarded and deaf, who was cared for away from home). The Austens were far from rich, and to supplement his income George Austen prepared boys for university, tutoring them in his home. Still, they lived comfortably enough. There seems to have been money for books (an expensive luxury), and the family kept horses and a carriage, an important mark of status.

Gentry

By manners and education, as well as by George Austen's profession and the careers chosen by his sons (the navy, the church, banking), the family could legitimately claim to be gentry, while background and income were at least "respectable"—a key word in the social vocabulary of the time and in Austen's novels. (One son, Edward, was adopted by distant, childless relatives—a wealthy land-owning family—taking their name and eventually inheriting their estate.) The two brothers in the navy would spend much of their time at sea during the long wars with France, but contact was never broken. That family background no doubt accounts for Austen's enthusiastic and knowledgeable presentation of naval affairs and characters, which is not only essential to the action of *Mansfield Park* and *Persuasion* but brings a sense of the greater world into both novels. Not only do her characterizations go well beyond popular stereotypes of the plain, bluff seaman, but she understood as well the difficulties of promotion, the role of luck, and the reward for success in terms of prizes captured and fortunes made.

In late eighteenth-century England, boys of the Austens' class might hope to go to university, or begin training for their profession, but unless the family was wealthy enough to afford a governess, girls could expect at most a few years away from home at a boarding school to pick up what knowledge they could. Throughout the nineteenth century Austen's range of knowledge would be consistently underestimated by her critics, no doubt because she had never been to university and consequently lacked the first-hand knowledge of Greek and Latin classics that was then considered essential to an educated person. No woman, and comparatively few men, could have been considered educated by that standard.

From 1785 to 1787, Jane and her sister, Cassandra, attended a boarding school for girls, the Abbey School in Reading. When she came home formal education had ended, but learning had not. Women of the upper classes usually received some training in music and art, the amount and quality depending largely on the family's wealth. The young Austen acquired several of the proper female "accomplishments"—she sang, she played the piano reasonably well, she did not paint or draw but was proud of her skill at sewing and embroidery, and she greatly enjoyed dancing. Ballroom scenes would be of crucial importance in her novels, but none of her heroines is notable for "accomplishments." More important, for a future author, her father's substantial library was open to her, apparently without restriction. (Family libraries provided an essential source of education for female writers in the nineteenth century.) The Austens were not only a lively and affectionate family, but an unusually literate one as well. . . .

Marriage

Yet it does not seem likely that a girl in that time and place would have deliberately set out to become a professional writer. Marriage was a woman's goal and fulfillment, it was a woman's career—a doctrine accepted by all of Austen's heroines, even Marianne Dashwood of *Sense and Sensibility*, who defies so many social conventions. And while waiting for marriage, Austen paid visits, she flirted, she danced ("There were twenty dances and I danced them all," she wrote to Cassandra in 1798. "I could just as well dance for a week together.") Like most girls of her day, she expected to marry, and one not entirely reliable recollection describes her as "the prettiest, silliest, most affected husband-hunting butterfly" that the writer had ever known.

Ultimately, marriage did not come to Jane Austen. We can guess that her intelligence, as well as her lack of fortune, might have put off some men, but we know comparatively little of Austen's emotional life. There may have been no intimate secrets to reveal, or they may have been lost by the time James Austen-Leigh came to write a memoir of his aunt's life—the first biography—more than 50 years after her death. But if there had been such secrets, he would not have published them. His *Memoir of Jane Austen* is a model of Victorian discretion. And whatever revelations Austen's correspondence might have contained were lost when Cassandra examined the letters after her sister's death and burned everything she considered too private or personal for public purview. Cassandra herself became engaged, but her fiancé died of fever in the West Indies. She too remained single, and the sisters' relationship would become the closet, most significant of their lives. . . .

Bath and Courtship

In 1801, George Austen retired with his wife and daughters to Bath, where he died several years later. It was an unhappy time for his younger daughter, who missed her old friends and relations and could not accustom herself to town life. (Bath becomes a background, rather unfavorably presented, in two of Austen's novels—*Northanger Abbey* and *Persuasion*.) Austen was 27 at the time of that move, and an opportunity for marriage seems to have come her way that summer, only to be snatched away. Details are uncertain, but apparently while at a seaside village in Devon, she met a charming, intelligent, and unmarried clergyman. They were instantly and strongly attracted to each other, but soon the man was called away, leaving Austen expecting a proposal by letter. Instead, word came a few weeks later that he had died in a sudden illness.

A few months afterward, while visiting friends in December 1801, Austen accepted a proposal of marriage from Harris Bigg-Wither, an awkward, stammering young man of 21 who was a landowner. Instead of facing a possible future of genteel poverty, she could become the mistress of a great house, in a countryside that she loved. Unfortunately, as she almost immediately recognized, she and young Bigg-Wither were hopelessly incompatible, and the next morning she broke the engagement, surely realizing that she would probably never have another chance to marry. There is no evidence of any future romance or offer of marriage.

Perhaps in consequence of that surely painful and embarrassing event, the age of 27 seems to have acquired a special significance for Austen. The 17-year-old Marianne Dashwood declares, in *Sense and Sensibility*, that a "woman of seven-and-twenty can never hope to feel or inspire affection." In *Pride and Prejudice* Charlotte Lucas, 27 and like Austen facing the specter of spinsterhood, saves herself from that fate by marrying the foolish Mr. Collins, declaring in justification, "I am not romantic, you know." . . .

Writing as Vocation

George Austen died early in 1805, but his wife and daughters stayed in Bath for two more years, with a drastically diminished income. In 1808 there was a temporary move to Southampton, where they expected to live with Jane's brother Frank, who planned to marry and make his home there. But a better solution soon presented itself. In 1809, Jane Austen's brother Edward, now a great landowner, gave his mother and sisters a cottage in the village of Chawton, 50 miles southwest of London and near his estate of Godmersham. (Restored by the Jane Austen Society, the house is today open to visitors.)

There, Austen would live quietly until a few months before her death in 1817, enjoying again the security of a true home, with country walks, village society, household duties, and occasional visits to brother Henry, a London banker, and to Edward and his family at Godmersham. Nephews and nieces began to provide a substitute for the family life at Steventon. Now, in the physical and emotional security of Chawton—conditions that seem to have been essential for her work—Austen began to write seriously again. . . .

No doubt encouraged by the publication of *Sense and Sensibility* and surely delighting in her own renewed creativity, Austen turned next to "First Impressions," revising it and retitling it *Pride and Prejudice*. Published in the winter of 1813, it too was well received. If it could not make readers weep and offered no harrowing adventures, then its wit and its realism offered compensation. There can be deep feeling in Austen's books, but there is little crying—her sales might have been better if she had made her readers weep. As for the author, the book was "her own darling child" and its heroine, Elizabeth Bennet, "as delightful a creature as ever appeared in print"—a judgment that generations of readers have agreed with. *Pride and Prejudice* brought the author £110 (this time she had sold the copyright instead of receiving royalties) and went through two more editions in the next four or five years. Her lifetime earnings from her writing would come to about £600. This was a significant amount, particularly for a woman, at a time when a skilled workman could support a family on considerably less than £100 a year, although not to be compared with the fortunes earned by her famous contemporaries, [George Gordon Byron, Lord] Byron and [Sir Walter] Scott. . . .

The Chawton years (1809–17) had been productive by any standard, yielding three novels carefully revised and three new novels written, two of these (*Emma* and *Mansfield Park*) long and complex works. All of this was done under conditions that would paralyze many writers. Austen had no room of her own at Chawton, writing instead, as Austen-Leigh tells us in his *Memoir*, in the common sitting room, subject to interruptions from casual visitors, when the manuscript would be whisked out of sight or hidden under a sheet of blotting paper. The hinge of an outer door was never oiled, so that its creaking could warn her of visitors. Her authorship was hardly a secret, but she preferred it to be known to as few people as possible. Such inconveniences surely made composition difficult at times, but Austen's situation had advantages—the security and the support, both economically and psychologically, that she enjoyed—which clearly outweighed its drawbacks.

Still, Austen must have had a remarkable ability to resist distraction to accomplish so much. If *Emma* was completed in only 14 months, she must have been writing several hours a day for most of those days and thinking about her work in progress for much of the remaining time. She was no genteel amateur in those Chawton years, as women were expected to be and as Austen-Leigh's *Memoir* often makes her seem, but a busy and highly productive writer, deeply concerned with the publication and reception of her work—a professional, in the full sense of the term.

What Class Meant for Women

Marilyn Butler

Marilyn Butler, a British literary critic and former rector of Exeter College, is the author of Romantics, Rebels, and Reactionaries: English Literature and Its Background, 1760-1830 *(1982).*

Jane Austen's father's social and economic situation forced the family to live modestly and to place their hopes for the future of their children on the kindness of wealthier relatives. Austen's brief formal schooling, her reading of the Lady's Magazine, *and her cousin Eliza taught her the fine points of manners expected of genteel young ladies.* Pride and Prejudice, *initially written under the title "First Impressions", was intended as a comedy of village society with an independent-minded young lady as its heroine. A few readers of the time of publication found Elizabeth disagreeable because of her disrespectful responses to her "betters," especially Lady Catherine and Darcy. The novel is also a portrait of the militia, a class of young officers who were known for their wild and irresponsible escapades and, in reality, justifiably rioted in Oxfordshire. Despite her own parents' seemingly happy marriage, Austen's own brief courtship with a man for whom she had feelings, and her overnight engagement to another man, she never married and does not often portray happy marriages in her fiction.*

Austen, Jane (1775–1817), novelist, was born on 16 December 1775 at the rectory in Steventon, near Basingstoke, Hampshire, the seventh child and younger daughter of George Austen (1731–1805), rector of Deane and Steventon and private tutor, and his wife, Cassandra (1739–1827), youngest daughter of the Revd Thomas Leigh (1696–1764) and Jane Walker (d. 1768).

Limited Means, Modest Rank

George Austen and his wife each inherited about £1000 during their early married years. With a growing family they moved in 1768 to the Steventon rectory, but found that they were living beyond their means. Immediate help came from a legacy left by Cassandra's mother, which her brother, James Leigh-Perrot, a trustee, released for the couple to invest. In 1773 George decided to take boys 'of good family' as boarders, preparing them for university, where they would meet a largely classical syllabus. Meanwhile his wife kept a bull and cows and grew vegetables in order to feed their large household. Cheerful and optimistic like her husband, Cassandra lacked formal education but had a homespun wit, and for thirty years managed her domestic world competently and energetically.

Jane Austen was born a month later than her parents expected; like the other Austen children, she was baptized at Steventon rectory on the day of her birth by George Austen. The formal ceremony took place on 5 April 1776 at St Nicholas's Church, which stood on the rising ground behind the rectory. The Austens' resident children divided into two groups. The three eldest boys (not counting George) commanded respect from the younger ones and were being prepared, like their father and maternal grandfather, for Oxford University. The boys qualified, on Cassandra's side, as 'founder's kin' at St John's College, which entitled them against competition to free tuition.

At the Abbey House School she amused herself as her socially mixed classmates did in following the adventures and trials of modern woman, as these were purveyed most readily and cheaply in a handful of specialist magazines, such as George Robinson's monthly miscellany, the *Lady's Magazine* (established 1770). In his first issue Robinson boasted that he catered for the widest possible range of taste, status, and income, from a duchess to a newly literate housemaid. In each issue from a quarter to a third of the space was likely to be occupied by fiction, much of it sent in by readers, who might set their narratives in stylized exotic worlds or in common domestic life among the middling sort. But the standard plotline for most longer fiction, whether published in multivolume book form or serialized in a magazine, was the courtship of lovers of unequal rank and means, involving the woman particularly in picaresque adventures and trials, with a happy ending always in jeopardy from the economic and social differences between the protagonists. Austen's first three novels conform to these archetypal features of the fiction of the 1780s and 1790s. At the age of eleven, however, Jane Austen was not concerned with novels but with reinstating herself among the people and activities of the crowded rectory at Steventon.

Jane Austen, her sister, and even her brother Henry 'came out' socially while under the wing of their exotic cousin Eliza.

Searching? For a Legacy

In summer 1788 the Steventon Austens decided that it would be a timely gesture to visit George's uncle and boyhood patron 'Old Francis' Austen.

With scant further prospects of a legacy from Kent, Jane's parents seriously turned their attention in the 1790s to the nearest of the Oxfordshire Leigh connections, Mrs Austen's childless brother, James Leigh-Perrot, and his wife, Jane, *née* Cholmeley, heiress of a Lincolnshire family of Atlantic traders long resident and prominent in Barbados. In 1793 their parents pressed Jane and Cassandra in vain to visit the couple in Bath. In the privacy of letters to Cassandra in the 1790s and 1800s, Jane often showed reluctance to visit unfamiliar cousins, such as her mother's connections the literary Cookes of Great Bookham. Fanny Burney, then Austen's favourite contemporary author, was living there in a picturesque area close to Boxhill. It had become a refuge for French aristocrats fleeing the revolution. Germaine de Staël, her lover Narbonne, and General D'Arblay, who married Burney in July 1793, visited Bookham at this time. Jane still felt shy at parties full of strangers and, now that she paid visits every second year at least to her brother Edward in Kent, she was made keenly aware of the social gap between 'East Kent wealth' and economies at the Steventon rectory. 'Kent is the only place for happiness. Everybody is rich there', she wrote sourly to Cassandra (*Letters*, 28), and, when her parents moved to a yet more unfashionable early dinner hour, 'half after Three . . . I am afraid you will despise us' (ibid., 27).

Publication of *Pride and Prejudice*

In August 1796 Jane visited her brother Edward and his wife, Elizabeth, at their first home, a large farmhouse at Rowling in Kent. It was while there, or immediately after returning home that October, that she began *Pride and Prejudice* under the title 'First Impressions', perhaps as an instinctive reaction against Kent hauteur. The author was the same age as her heroine Elizabeth Bennet at the start of composition ('not one and twenty'). This, the first of her novels to be completed, was finished in August 1797, and offered by her father to the publisher Thomas Cadell on 1 November 1797 as a novel in three volumes 'about the length of Miss Burney's '*Evelina*' (Austen-Leigh, Memoir, chap. 8). The publisher declined without asking to see the manuscript. 'First Impressions' remained a family favourite, a fact confirmed by regular rereadings by Cassandra and Jane's close friend Martha Lloyd (*Letters*, 35, 44). The title had to be changed, however, after the publication of Margaret Holford's novel *First Impressions, or, The Portrait* in 1801. Austen replaced it with *Pride and Prejudice*, taking a phrase from Burney's *Cecilia* (1782) as her new title.

George Austen might have sought another publisher for Jane's 'First Impressions', but did not; Jane turned stoically to her other novel-in-waiting, the tale of the two sisters Elinor and Marianne. The treatment of scenes between two sympa-

Jane Austen learned the fine points of manners expected of genteel young ladies from reading Lady's Magazine, *her cousin Eliza, and her brief formal schooling.* Mansell/Time and Life Pictures/Getty Images.

thetic marriageable sisters in each of these early novels must in some way have been affected by the news of Tom's death that reached Steventon about 1 May 1797, while Jane still had the closing chapters of *Pride and Prejudice* to write. But Jane seemed already to have a policy of observing the conventions of two types of stage comedy—witty or 'laughing' comedy, and the comedy of sentiment, which is likely to include pathos and touches of tragedy. Each mode had its appropriate heroine, a tender melancholic romantic for the comedy of sentiment, and conversely an independent-minded woman of the world for laughing comedy. Another convention observable in the theatre governs minor characters, and this too Austen observes in her early pair of novels; the comic minor characters in *Pride and Prejudice*, Mrs Bennet, Mr Collins, Lady Catherine, are broader and much more developed than their equivalents in *Sense and Sensibility*, Sir John Middleton, Mrs Jennings, Mrs Palmer, and Miss Steele.

For her laughing comedy 'First Impressions' Austen looked for an outstanding heroine in the stage tradition of comedy and farce of the 1780s, and understandably borrowed from Eliza de Feuillide's favourite, the warm, mature, and generous Lady Bell Bloomer in Cowley's *Which is the Man?*. Lizzie Bennet, unheroically placed as the second of five sisters, has the intelligence of Cowley's Letitia and Lady Bell. She even takes on a similar leading role in her own domestic world, which is anarchic thanks to the idleness of her father and the limited capacities of her mother. Lizzie stands up to the uncivil Darcy and his flatterer, Miss Bingley, and loyally champions her elder sister Jane's depth of feeling for Bingley. Female camaraderie of this type was also a central theme of Susanna Centlivre's play *The Wonder*.

But the relationship Austen develops between Lizzie and Darcy has a nearer model in Roxalana, heroine of Bickerstaff's farce *The Sultan*, one of the last plays acted at Steventon late in 1788. Roxalana is a sensible, self-reliant Englishwoman, unfazed by finding herself in the harem of a sultan who comes to prefer her stout advice to that of the cronies and flatterers at his court. She is by no means aristocratic, as Cowley's heroines are, but of the trading class. Osmyn the vizier reflects on this after her triumph: 'who would have thought that a little cock'd-up nose would have overturn'd the customs of a mighty empire!' (act 2) In fact, though *Pride and Prejudice* was recognized as a fine comedy in the mainstream tradition and was a runaway success on publication in 1813, a minority of readers throughout the nineteenth century could not stomach Lizzie's vulgar mother and aunt, still less her own pert answers to Darcy and to his aunt Lady Catherine.

The XXXX Historical Context

Unusually for Austen the novel is also grounded in real-life public events: southern England at the outset of a major war, when threatened with a French invasion. The circumstances are the arrival in county towns of regiments of militia from other regions, following France's declaration of war in February 1793. By the winter of 1794–5 three such regiments—the South Devonshires, Oxfordshires, and Derbyshires—were billeted in counties near north Hampshire, and they caused trouble locally through riotousness, drunkenness, lechery, and bad debts. Their senior officers were either professional soldiers or gentlemen but the men and junior officers were inexperienced and, like Lieutenant Wickham in *Pride and Prejudice*, might be disreputable. Jane's brother Henry, though intended for the church, had enlisted in the Oxfordshire militia, which was mostly billeted further south in Hampshire. Gregarious and socially ambitious, Henry fed Jane with tales about the different militias; the South Devonshires, available for her to meet in Basingstoke nearby; the superior rank and wealth of the Derbyshires' officers, which ensured good billets in the county town of Hertford (the novel's Meryton); and the debacle the Oxfordshires experienced when, in the freezing winter of 1794–5, they moved to new unready barracks near Brighton and rioted to such effect that the regulars and subsequently the courts had to deal with them.

Snobs and Rascals

Jane Austen's enhanced social understanding of her southern English world went deeper than the mere act of tracing the movements of soldiers on the map. Disguised by their uniform, handsome young men turned out to be villains and could wreck a family's peace. *Pride and Prejudice* is a story full of movement and instability, thanks partly to the dastardly escapades of Wickham with Georgiana Darcy at Ramsgate and with Lydia Bennet at Brighton and London, and eventually as a junior officer in the regulars at Newcastle. But it also pencils in respectable social gradations, as in the case of the worthy Gardiners, the kind of City of London couple who in real life were business associates at this time of the Austen cousins, moving into mansions near Sevenoaks. To match Mr Darcy's concessions to the City, Lizzie travels to Derbyshire, is admitted to Pemberley as a mere tourist, and learns from the housekeeper that Darcy is not seen at home as an arrogant snob or despot, but as a good-natured boy who has grown up to be a protective affectionate brother. The successful weave of the many strands of this ambitious plot is one of the causes of its lasting charm.

There are signs of Jane Austen's sisterly concern and shared grieving with Cassandra in the later dialogues between Jane and Lizzie Bennet in 'First Impressions' and, more extensively, in *Sense and Sensibility* in Elinor's tender concern for her sister Marianne when she loses Willoughby and falls seriously ill. Jane Bennet is only a secondary heroine in *Pride and Prejudice*, but she fits all the stereotyped features of the classic sentimental heroine: beautiful, virtuous, domestic, and reticent. Like so many heroines, she appears to have lost her lover, Bingley, after she is traduced by his sisters, false friends to Jane, and by Darcy. When Jane thinks Bingley has gone, she stoically performs her domestic duties, as Cassandra did in Kent through her early adulthood. Family relationships and above all sisterhood are regular features of Austen's novels, but the emotion generated by a sympathetic sister's share in another's pain at the loss of a lover is more sustained and raw in these two novels of the 1790s than anywhere else in her work.

Austen's Engagement

A week after their arrival, on the evening of Thursday 2 December, Jane Austen accepted a proposal of marriage from Harris Bigg-Wither, the Bigg sisters' younger brother.

If she had gone through with a marriage to this stuttering, awkward man, six years younger than herself, Jane Austen at twenty-seven could have housed and provided for her parents, who were facing a fairly straitened old age in lodgings at Bath, and Cassandra too if she wished it. On the death of his father, Harris Bigg-Wither would have inherited Manydown, and Jane would have become its mistress. She was already comfortable in the house and with its attractive owners. But there were problems at Manydown. Harris did not get on with his father, and really wanted to remove himself with Jane or another wife to a home of his own. For whatever reason, Jane thought better of her acceptance overnight, and early the following morning she and Cassandra departed precipitately for Steventon to save further embarrassment. After a brief explanation to James and Mary, they returned with James to Bath on 4 December.

It was, however, the nearest Jane Austen appears to have come to marriage. In her youth she enjoyed flirting as much as she enjoyed dancing. But it was the era in her life when she was seeing much of Eliza, another witty woman who loved to tease but also meant to retain her independence even after her marriage, in December 1797, to Jane's brother Henry, Eliza's first husband having been executed in France in 1794. After Jane's death, Cassandra told the nieces the story of a man Jane met on holiday in a south-west resort in the early 1800s, who appeared seriously attached to Jane, as she was to him; they never saw him again, and only later discovered that he had died. Much the same story was retold in Sir Francis Hasting Doyle's *Reminiscences and Opinions* (1886) as emanating from a resident of Chawton, though on this occasion the lovelorn suitor was encountered by the Austens on a mythical trip to

Switzerland during the peace of Amiens. In either version the tale has the flavour of Cassandra's making rather than Jane's.

Except in the case of the Crofts in *Persuasion*, Austen in her fiction is hesitant about the long-term satisfactions of marriage. Older couples, the Sir Thomas Bertrams, the Allens, and the Bennets, have long since forgotten youthful rapture, if they ever experienced it.

Social Critic

Jane Austen emerged between 1870 and 1960 as a social critic, a moralist, an incomparable artist, and latterly a popular and universal writer. Today her novels are firm favourites among book buyers and library users and feature prominently in polls of favourite fiction, with a special attachment to *Pride and Prejudice*. It was the relatively recent recognition of Austen's universality that drove the rapid growth in the 1990s of hotly competing television and film adaptations of all six of her finished novels. 1995 was a particularly notable year, with an ambitious, well-cast, and conscientiously researched *Pride and Prejudice* made for television, with running time of five hours, produced by Sue Birtwistle and scripted by Andrew Davies, a team that had already succeeded with George Eliot's *Middlemarch* the preceding year. The production was deliberately literary, and committed to delivering the inward interest and complex relationships of nineteenth-century novels.

Pride and Prejudice
and Class Issues

Levels of Rank

David Spring

David Spring edited European Landed Elites in the Nineteenth
Century *(1977) and, with Eileen Spring,* Ecology and Religion
in History *(1974).*

David Spring explains that the world of Pride and Prejudice,
*while it may not encompass many different social ranks and re-
gions, does present an accurate portrayal of class within the
world of the rural "neighborhood," restricted to village leaders,
not to its working-class citizens, who are described as being "in a
low line." Critics have labeled the neighborhood variously as the
middle class, the rural gentry, and the bourgeoisie (defined as an
uncultured middle class obsessed with money). But the neighborhood actually contained the landed gentry who were comfortably
situated, the gentry with little money, and the unlanded gentry.
The last owned less than 400 acres. The unlanded gentry, like
Elizabeth Bennet's family, were also often called the pseudo-
gentry. Spring contends that these three class groups in the neighborhood were usually not in conflict because they depended on
one another, and often the landed gentry accepted the pseudo-
gentry into their ranks by means of financial success or marriage.*

The method of this essay will be to group and assess opinions about Jane Austen's society under various heads. I
will begin with those students, relatively few but of high distinction, who find that in having no comprehensive view of
society she in fact portrays no real society. One such student
thus argues that she portrays an idyll. Another argues that her
society, although in a sense real, is hardly more than an extended family.

The Real England

The first is best represented by Lionel Trilling in a remarkable essay on *Emma*. He wrote there that "any serious historian will make it sufficiently clear that the real England was not the England of her novels, except as it gave her license to imagine the England which we call hers." . . .

It is not, of course, especially rewarding to speculate why Trilling delivered himself of this judgment. Plainly enough it has failed to convince—and, I would think, for good reasons.

One is that [according to J. Bayley] a "serious historian" would be hard put to make much of "*the* real England." He is more likely to think of several real Englands coexisting. Admittedly Jane Austen's was not the England of the Durham coal miners, or of plain-living aesthetes like the Wordsworths, or of London shopkeepers like Francis Place, or of London bohemians like the Prince Regent—to name but a few of the real Englands. Instead, her England was that of the local rural elite. She called it "neighborhood"—one of the prime words in her social vocabulary. She meant by it not the tenant farmers, the rural laborers, the country-house servants, or the village tradesmen. They did not belong to the world of neighborhood. Rather she meant by neighborhood their social superiors, who lived in large houses and whose dining, dancing, and marrying provided the substance of her stories.

A second reason for skepticism is Jane Austen's social vocabulary—one that fits her world of the rural elite. This vocabulary, however, is something different from the modern (largely nineteenth-century) language of class. Perhaps only on one occasion—in *Persuasion*—does she make use of the language of class, and even there it strikes the modern eye as a bit stilted and odd. Otherwise the reader finds no "working class," "middle class," or "upper class"—or any of the variations on these that the nineteenth century produced. This is perhaps understandable, given that the language of class had as a major (if implicit) assumption that society was becoming relatively fluid. Jane Austen, however, had no great liking for social fluidity. . . .

The Language of Class

What, then, is her social language? "Neighborhood" has already been noted as comprising the rural elite. Expressions like "the very great," or "resident landholder," or "profession" designate groups within that elite—all of them covered by the word "gentleman." For those parts of society in varying degree inferior to her elite she uses a variety of expressions such as "the second rate and third rate," or "half gentlemen," or, for the very lowest, "the poor." Or she may specify these inferiors as "yeomen," "laborers," "tenant farmers," or "in trade"—all of them, as she would say, "in a low line." The word "line"—like such words as "sphere," "circle," or "rank"—does some of the work that the language of class would do later to indicate large divisions within society. All this would suggest that Jane Austen was not bereft of a notion of social reality, although it may be unlike our own. . . .

Social Types

That Jane Austen's novels deal with little more than an extended family has a bit of plausibility: we are all familiar with her advice to her novel-writing niece: "Three or four families in a Country Village is the very best thing to work on." But her families exemplify a variety of social types, all of which go to make up a larger society, the nature of which she is clearly aware of. They do not exist in a social vacuum. Even Simpson admits that she was a close student of a least one social type—although his assertion that only sailors were the successful object of her studies would seem to be farfetched.

After all, her domestic opportunities for the study of social types were not confined to sailors. If two brothers were sailors, two were parsons; so was her father, as well as numerous friends and relations. Another brother was a large-acred Kentish and Hampshire landowner, and both in Steventon and Chawton the gentry families were well known to her. Nor is it really clear that she understood sailors better than she understood parsons or landowners or soldiers (her favorite brother, Henry, was once a soldier as well as a failed banker before he rushed precipitately into the church). Indeed, a case might be made that her sailors are in some ways the least convincing of the social types in her novels. . . .

Naming the Bennets' Social Class

It would be fair to say that the bulk of Jane Austen interpreters have had no trouble in agreeing that the world of her novels is real, a part of the real England. But they have had trouble in agreeing on what to call it, on how to characterize it. In the course of more than a century and a half, Jane Austen interpretation has boxed the compass of social respectability. It began by describing her as the annalist of the "middle classes," of "ordinary and middle life." Later she was said to be the aristocracy's annalist, or more commonly the gentry's. Most recently interpretation seems to have turned back to its beginnings and plumped for a bourgeois Jane Austen.

High on the list of reasons for calling Jane Austen's society bourgeois, it would seem, is the ubiquity of money in her novels. Things and persons seem all to have their price. Even naval officers go to sea in a great war to make money. This pervasive monetarization of the novels was in itself perhaps enough to catch the eye of literary critics. But there were also historians, looking to other evidence than the novel, who reinforced this conclusion. So influential an historian as R.H. Tawney, in his famous essay on the gentry, characterized sixteenth- and seventeenth-century landowners as bourgeois because they were more intent on making money than their predecessors. . . .

Two well-dressed eighteenth-century gentlemen, in a lavishly decorated room, illustrates the life of landed gentry, so central to Pride and Prejudice. Mansell/Time & Life Pictures/Getty Images.

Not surprisingly, the bourgeois label found wide acceptance. But some critics have had their doubts. Graham Hough, for example, observed in 1970 that the bourgeoisie was "too blunt an instrument to have much explanatory value." And almost two decades earlier, in one of those revealing footnotes where professors choose to argue with themselves, Marvin

Mudrick said almost as much. His admission is especially interesting, for in the text of the same book he came down heavily on the bourgeois nature of Jane Austen's novels. He wrote there, for example, of "the particularities of bourgeois courtship," meaning by this its monetary aspects. . . .

A Hybrid Class

The world of neighborhood, the world of the rural elite, was indeed hybrid, hence the disagreement on what to call it. Strictly speaking, it contained three groups, two of which—the landed aristocracy and gentry—were less distinctive one from the other than both were from the third group. What brought them close together was the ownership of landed estates. They made their money in the same way—mainly by letting land to tenant farmers. . . .

Where the aristocracy and gentry chiefly differed was in what—to use one of her favorite phrases—Jane Austen called "style of living," that is, in their status, in how they spent their money.

Money and Standing

Aristocratic landowners, having more money, had more to spend. A few had a great deal more to spend, as much as £100,000 of gross income' annually. To appreciate what a very great deal this was, remember that in the first decade of the nineteenth century a skilled worker with a family to support would have been fortunate to enjoy an annual income of £100, an unskilled worker of £40. Even the lowest annual income of an aristocratic landowner was something like £5,000 to £10,000, Mrs. Bennet's measurement of the lordly life. Aristocratic incomes, therefore, made for splendid status: great houses, great estates (perhaps several), great parks, a house in London, a seat or seats in the House of Commons for sons and relations, a hereditary seat in the House of Lords for titled fathers, perhaps a position at Court. Like the gentry, the aristocracy had local roots, but they also enjoyed a more metropolitan existence. They were less likely to marry locally: they traveled more, as Elizabeth Bennet once suggested to Darcy, up to London, and among "a range of great families."

The gentry had less money to spend—although relative to the income of a working man, even modest gentry incomes were still impressive, probably on a level with the income of a large town merchant and exceeding the incomes of most professional men. A modest gentry income was something like £1,000 to £2,000 a year. It was Mr. Bennet's income in *Pride and Prejudice*, Colonel Brandon's in *Sense and Sensibility....*

To the unpleasant but aristocratic Lady Catherine de Bourgh, even Mr. Bennet's Longbourn with its £2,000 a year was scarcely adequate: deficient in park, servants, and whatever else was needed to impose on the imaginations of social inferiors. But these modest gentry estates, covering England in their thousands, managed to supply their owners with comfort and status sufficient to make them the natural leaders of their local communities. Assisted principally by the resident Anglican clergy, they ran their parishes and counties, acting as overseers of the poor, and as magistrates. They were more at home in the local county town than in London's West End.

Of the two, gentry and aristocracy, Jane Austen preferred the former. Not that she was uncritical of the gentry....

But socially she stood closer to the gentry than to the aristocracy, especially to the smaller-incomed gentry. Morally she approved of their more settled habits, of their less ostentatious patterns of consumption, of their limited capacity—compared with that of the Court aristocracy led by the Prince Regent—to perpetrate a national scandal. Her novels are thus not much populated with aristocratic figures. Moreover, when they appear, they are almost invariably silly, both men and women....

The Nonlanded

Strictly speaking, then, Jane Austen belonged to neither of the first two groups in that hybrid world of the rural elite—neither to the aristocracy nor to the gentry—but to a third group, so far unnamed. This group comprised the nonlanded: the professional and rentier families, first and foremost the Anglican clergy; second, other professions like the law—preferably barristers rather than solicitors—and the fighting services; and last, the rentiers recently or long retired from business. I have described them as nonlanded, by which I mean that if they owned land, and doubtless many of them owned some, they owned comparatively little, perhaps 100 acres and less. Sometimes they merely rented a house and its adjoining land, as did the Bingleys in *Pride and Prejudice*; and often, notably in the case of the Anglican parson, they held land (and sometimes farmed it) for life. By and large, they were neither lords of manors nor collectors of rent from tenant farmers. But they lived in big houses, held or owned enough land to assure privacy. . . .

This third group, the nonlanded, is the one most likely to be described by Jane Austen interpreters as bourgeois—although some (as we have seen) have also described the entire world of neighborhood as bourgeois. The word, however, ill suits both the smaller as well as the larger social unit. For bourgeois evokes an urban—or at least an actively trading—milieu. It also evokes a degree of social hostility—of class antagonism, to use the Marxist phrase—that was also inappropriate to the several groups within the world of neighborhood. There were tensions within that world, but these were something different from the deeply divided outlook of class antagonism. . . .

The pseudo-gentry were "pseudo" because they were not landowners in the same sense as the gentry and aristocracy were. They cannot be said to have owned landed estates. But they were gentry of a sort, primarily because they sought strenuously to be taken for gentry. They devoted their lives to acquiring the trappings of gentry status for themselves and especially their children: the schooling, the accent, the manners (from style of conversation to dressing for dinner), the sports, the religion, the habit of command, the large house in its own grounds, servants, carriages and horses, appropriate husbands and wives, and, last but not least, an appropriate income, which Jane Austen called "independence," that most desirable of all social states. In short they had a sharp eye for the social escalators, were skilled in getting on them, and (what was more important) no less skilled in staying on them. . . .

The World of Neighborhood

Let me conclude with these reflections. On the matter of Jane Austen's world of neighborhood, it is important to keep in mind how peculiarly English a world this was. It is unlikely that European landed elites had so close a relation with a part of the so-called bourgeois world as the English landed elite had with its pseudo-gentry, or that the pseudo-gentry in European societies was so formidable a phenomenon as the English. Both Matthew Arnold and Alexis de Tocqueville suggested that this was the case. This would mean that social historians must walk more warily than they have done—as must students of society generally, whether they be literary critics indulging in social discourse or social scientists indulging in historical speculation.

Historians have been fond of viewing social change dramatically—and in the English case this has helped mislead interpreters of Jane Austen's world. For that world did not function dramatically. Its component groups, landowners and pseudo-gentry, were not in collision. The former provided the pseudo-gentry with what sociologists call a reference group— that is, a model for their lifestyle as well as with jobs of all sorts. In turn the pseudo-gentry provided the landowners with ideas and specialized capacities and services. If the several groups had a common name, it was that of gentleman.

Rank and Human Relationships

Thomas Keymer

Thomas Keymer, Elmore fellow and tutor of English at St. Anne's College, Oxford, is the author of Sterne, the Moderns, and the Novel *(2002).*

Thomas Keymer gives the reader of Pride and Prejudice *a complex and detailed version of class characteristics and practices in context. He explains that the structure used by Jane Austen in* Pride and Prejudice, *for example, predates the work and language of late eighteenth-century and early nineteenth-century novelists of reform. A writer in 1753, almost twenty-five years before Austen's birth, listed five classes: nobility, gentry, genteel trades, common trades, and peasantry. The concepts of class and rank in* Pride and Prejudice *had slightly different shades of meaning. Class had more to do with productivity and income, while rank referred more to lineage. The neighborhood classes, reflected in the novel, amounted to about 26,000 males, or a little more than 1 percent of the population. The most valuable information gleaned from Keymer's article is the situation of Darcy among a landowning, untitled class who regarded "Mr." as a badge of honor, a moral place beyond politics and the struggle for title and higher rank.*

Social position is of consuming importance in the novels [of Jane Austen], with individuals and families measuring their relative standings to the finest degree while devising long-term strategies for advancement in status. Yet these concerns are articulated in terms predating the class-based language of politics that grew up among radicals such as [Tho-

Thomas Keymer, *Jane Austen in Context*. New York: Cambridge University Press, 2005. Copyright © 2005 Cambridge University Press. Reprinted with the permission of Cambridge University Press.

mas] Paine, [Thomas] Spence and [John] Thelwall in the 1790s, became consolidated in the work of social theorists such as Robert Owen and David Ricardo in the 1810s and 1820s, and continues to shape modern assumptions. The term 'class' was already current by Austen's day—P.J. Corfield cites a writer of 1753 who itemised English society in 'five Classes; *viz.* the Nobility, the Gentry, the genteel Trades (all those particularly which require large Capital), the common Trades, and the Peasantry'—but as an organising concept it was yet to diverge significantly from traditional specifications of rank, station or degree. 'Rank' remained the established model, and dictated conventional thought. Where 'class' would be measured in terms above all of productivity and income, locating individuals in socio-economic positions attained through material success, 'rank' placed primary emphasis on lineage, implying that social status was more or less inalienably conferred by birth and descent. Where 'class' brings with it overtones of structural antagonism and conflict, moreover, 'rank' suggested stratifications that were harmonious, orderly and stable— ranks being nothing if not serried [notched]. . . . [S]ocial hierarchy was guaranteed by ties of interdependence and mutual advantage, and consisted of 'fixed, invariable external rules of distinction of rank, which create no jealousy, as they are allowed to be accidental' (i.e. given).

As exponents of a genre specialising in close and particular renderings of social reality, few novelists of Austen's day fail to register the defining importance of rank. Yet it is hard to think of a contemporary or precursor in whose fiction there is quite so thorough an immersion in, and calibration of, the minutiae of the system. The eighteenth-century novelist most admired by Jane Austen, Samuel Richardson, wrote innovatively about emerging fault-lines in the strata of rank, and in *Pamela* (1740)—in which a maid-servant wins her master's hand—he pioneered the plot of marital elevation that Austen was to use herself in more muted form. . . .

Jane Austen, by contrast [with Richardson], was native to this world [the gentry world], and writes with unfailing alertness to its codes and conventions. . . .

The Aristocracy

The dedication of *Emma* to the Prince Regent takes Austen's fiction to the very apex of the social pyramid, but otherwise the highest echelons of the nobility are thinly represented. Unlike the 'silver fork' novelists who dominated the fiction market of the 1820s with their voyeuristic depictions of high society, Austen's attitude to aristocratic manners is one of general neglect, punctuated by occasional disdain. . . . Austen thus ignores a group that continued to hold the reins of political power—peers and their sons formed a majority in every government cabinet between 1783 and 1835—and also the informal strings of patronage, connection and dependency that bound together the social hierarchy. Even so, aristocracy retains a teasing subliminal presence in Austen's cast. . . .

Beneath a peerage of three hundred or so families in England there ranged the graduated demographic on which Austen concentrates her gaze: a gentry society comprising the families of approximately (in 1803) 540 baronets, 350 knights, 6,000 landed squires and 20,000 gentlemen, amounting in total to about 1.4 per cent of the national population and enjoying 15.7 per cent of the national income. It is to this rurally based society, centred on major landowning families and descending in fine gradations through non-landed professionals and moneyed rentiers of varying status, that Austen's characters refer when they speak of the 'neighbourhood'. In each novel, 'neighbourhood' is a feature of both the landscape and its elite population. It denotes both the hierarchy of estates and manors that revolved around the local great house, and the rural gentry who inhabited these places, where they competed for visits from, and invitations to, houses on the level above, and made seasonal forays to London or Bath in pursuit of extended connection. Though rich in rivalries and tensions, this is a hierarchy still defined and united by vertical ties of influence and dependency down to its lowest reaches, and not yet acrimoniously fragmented—as in 'condition of England' novels of the 1840s—by horizontal solidarities of class. The cities might be another story, but as late as 1824 a representative essayist could still exult that the dangerous chasm between noble and labouring classes in other nations did not exist in England [according to David Robinson]: 'with us the space between the ploughman and the peer is crammed with circle after circle, fitted in the most admirable manner for sitting upon each other, for connecting the former with the latter, and for rendering the whole perfect in cohesion, strength and beauty'.

At the peak of this gentry society are the baronets, the lowest hereditary titled order, whom Austen represents with uneven levels of distinction. . . .

Women of High Rank

Women of higher rank incorporate their Christian names in a form that distinguishes Lady Catherine de Bourgh and Lady Anne Darcy, in *Pride and Prejudice*, as titled in their own right. Regardless of their marital status or the rank (if lower) of their husbands, daughters of peers invariably used this form, which marks out both Lady Catherine, the wife of a knight, and Lady Anne, the wife of a commoner, as noble by birth (in this case, as daughters of an earl). . . .

Rural Gentry and Darcy

Scarcely lower in standing were the greatest of the landowning commoners, who had not been touched by—or in some cases had eschewed—the titles of their ostensible superiors. With an estate worth more, at £10,000 a year, than that of many nobles, Mr Darcy represents an important category of rural gentry in Austen's England: men of wealth and lineage for whom plain

'Mr' was a badge of honour. A conspicuous instance is the great commoner Thomas William Coke, of Holkham in Norfolk, who inherited estates worth £12,000 in 1776 and improved their yield threefold by 1816, yet during this period twice refused ennoblement—a gesture that made even a marquis congratulate him on 'such independence, portraying a dignity of mind above all heraldry'. In this context, the note of regret with which Lady Catherine de Bourgh describes Darcy's paternal line as 'respectable, honourable, and ancient, though untitled' signals her distance from the Tory values often attributed to Jane Austen herself, according to which Darcy's untitled state might even be his highest distinction. Simple esquireship connotes an incorruptible aloofness from the processes of political ingratiation and meretricious reward that had characterised the Whig hegemony of the previous century—a 'peer-making age' (as one minor novelist put it) during which the House of Lords grew in size from 153 in 1688 to 224 in 1780, despite the natural extinction of titles over the same period. After 1780, the younger [William] Pitt's efforts to break the power of the Whig magnates led to increased rates of ennoblement, and brought into being a new body of parvenu peers [those who rose above their status at birth] who diluted the old equation between aristocratic rank and blue blood. Jane Austen's egregious kinsman Sir Egerton Brydges (Bart.) was among many traditionalists affronted, in this process, by Pitt's 'palpable preference of mercantile wealth, and by his inborn hatred of the old aristocracy'. . . .

Yet personal mobility of status was becoming more achievable as Austen wrote, and other novels reflect the mechanisms involved. Though peopled by conservative matriarchs like Mrs Ferrars and Lady Catherine, who seek 'to have the distinction of rank preserved' and promote strict endogamy [marriage within a social unit] to this end, the novels deal in more than mere romance in their characteristic endings, where traditional dynastic alliances give way to modern love matches.

Elizabeth is not a gentlewoman's daughter, and has an uncle in trade, but marries into the highest squirearchy [class of landed gentry]. . . . Other processes promoting the interpenetration of social layers arose from the Napoleonic Wars, which not only threw up new opportunities for trade and industry or for success in the profession of arms, but also conferred new prestige on leaders in either field. 'Mushrooms are every day starting up from the dunghill of trade', as [Robert] Southey lamented in 1806, so 'undermining the distinction of ranks in society'. Though Sir William Lucas remains cowed by old aristocracy, the confidence of the Bingleys in 'associating with people of rank' provides a bolder instance of entry into elite circles from the platform of trade. . . . For Harold Perkin, these processes of elevation and assimilation slowed the formation of a moneyed class at odds with the landed gentry, and harnessed local dynamism in the service of larger stability: 'the result was a self-contained system of social movement which left the shape and structure of society precisely as before, a "stationary state" based on the restless movement of its constituent atoms' (Perkin, *Modern English Society*, p. 62). Bourgeois revolution is not in prospect at Highbury, to be sure. If any threat exists, it lurks instead in the hidden ranks of the labouring—or, worse, non-labouring—poor, dissevered from gentry society by the decay of rural paternalism, and ominously ruffling its serene surface in the shape of gypsies and poultry thieves.

Courtship and Class

David Monaghan

Professor at Mount Saint Vincent University in Halifax, Nova Scotia, David Monaghan is the author of Jane Austen, Structure and Social Vision *(1980) and numerous articles on Canadian, American, and English novelists.*

In the following essay David Monaghan explains that Darcy and Elizabeth's courtship in Pride and Prejudice *is a story of negotiations between classes. He asserts that both of them harbor prejudices against the other's place in society. But after Darcy goes out of his way to help her family with Lydia, who has run away with Wickham, Elizabeth's prejudice begins to recede. The more Darcy sees of Elizabeth and the Gardiners (her aunt and uncle), the less biased he becomes. Monaghan contends that this change in bias permits the union between the two of them.*

Elizabeth Bennet is firmly located in a world of lesser gentry and bourgeoisie. Her father owns a small estate worth £2000 per annum, her mother is the daughter of an attorney, and her uncle, Mr Gardiner, is in trade. Darcy, on the other hand, belongs to the noble de Bourgh family, possesses the Pemberley estate, and has an income of £10,000 per annum, enough to put his among the four hundred most important families. Lacking any experience of the other's world, each relies on stereotypes; Elizabeth accepts the common view that aristocrats are worthless snobs, and Darcy believes that anyone connected with trade must be vulgar and unworthy of respect. Unfortunately, since Darcy's visit to Meryton beings him into contact with Mrs Bennet, and since Elizabeth witnesses Darcy's supercilious behavior at the Meryton ball, their first exposure to each other's worlds serves to confirm rather than disprove these stereotypes.

Social Stereotyping

Further acquaintance gives Darcy and Elizabeth opportunities to refine their crude social typecasting. And Darcy does indeed quickly come to see some of Elizabeth's virtues. However, instead of re-examining her milieu in the light of the fact that it has produced at least one admirable person, he simply tries to isolate Elizabeth from her background. In his dealings with Elizabeth, Darcy begins to behave politely, but he continues to express contempt for the Bennet family and the people of Meryton. By so doing, Darcy provides Elizabeth with plenty of evidence to confirm her prejudices. However, the way in which Elizabeth reacts to Darcy suggests that her feelings towards him have their origins in more than simple moral disapproval. Even at his worst Darcy is no more objectionable than Lady Catherine de Bourgh or Mr Collins, and he is certainly not as bad as Wickham is finally revealed to be. . . .

Darcy is not put off by Elizabeth's rudeness, and in fact seems to sense the emotions that lie beneath it. As he explains later, her behaviour was such as to make him anticipate the success of his first marriage proposal, and Elizabeth acknowledges the ambiguity of her response to him:

'I believed you to be wishing, expecting my addresses.'

'My manners must have been in fault, but not intentionally I assure you.'

Elizabeth's Class Prejudice

Therefore, in spite of his reservations about her background, Darcy makes many attempts to approach Elizabeth. Each time, Elizabeth rejects him. This creates an extremely frustrating situation and it is one that cannot be resolved until each has come to a better understanding of the other's social group. For all the attentions he pays her, Darcy will be unacceptable to Elizabeth so long as he fails to recognise that the gentry-middle class as a whole is worthy of his respect. And Elizabeth will continue to blind herself to Darcy's virtues until she has arrived at a fair estimation of the environment' which has shaped him. Darcy's meeting with the excellent Gardiners, whose gentility is not diminished by the fact that they live within sight of their warehouses, and Elizabeth's introduction to Pemberley, a place that epitomises the taste, importance and enormous social responsibilities of the nobility, are necessary prerequisites of personal reconciliation.

The social and the personal are so closely bound together in the relationship between Elizabeth and Darcy that the larger implications of the marriage into which they finally enter are very evident. In her other novels Jane Austen tends to suggest that the continued moral well-being of society depends on the ability of the gentry to ward off the disruptive influence of the middle class and the aristocracy. But *Pride and Prejudice* concludes with a union which grows directly out of the ability of the participants to recognize that, in spite of their different functions, the middle class, the gentry and the nobility are all committed to the ideal of concern for others. The materialism and vulgarity of the bourgeoisie are as much in evidence in *Pride and Prejudice* as they were in *Northanger Abbey* and *Sense and Sensibility* [two of Austen's other five published novels]. So is the snobbery of the aristocracy. But here people like Charlotte Lucas and Lady Catherine de Bourgh represent deviations from the norm of their groups rather than the norm itself.

Dancing and Acceptance

Since courtship contributes so much to the themes of *Pride and Prejudice*, it is appropriate that dancing, which is, as Henry Tilney points out, the courtship ritual *par excellence*, should play a major part in its structure. Four incidents involving invitations to dance lay the groundwork for a pattern of approach and rejection which serves as an emblem of Darcy's relationship with Elizabeth. Other dance invitations—Bingley's to Jane, Collins' to Elizabeth and Wickham's to Elizabeth—provide a commentary on the problems and misunderstandings that exist between Darcy and Elizabeth. The dance disappears from the novel after the Netherfield ball, and emphasis is transferred to the visit. By comparing her impressions of Rosings and Pemberley Elizabeth is finally able to achieve a proper understanding of the aristocracy. Darcy's perspective on the middle class is similarly broadened by his meetings with Mr Collins and Sir William Lucas at Rosings, and the Gardiners at Pemberley. Consequently the pattern of approach and rejection which was continued at Rosings is broken at Pemberley when Elizabeth accepts several invitations in rapid succession. These temporary polite unions promise something more permanent, and the final section of *Pride and Prejudice* is organised around three marriages, those between Lydia and Wickham, and Bingley and Jane, quite literally clearing the way for Darcy and Elizabeth's. . . .

Because he regards Meryton society as vulgar, Darcy refuses to recognise that it can claim even the minimum of good manners from him. When Mrs Long, who 'does not keep a carriage, and had come to the ball in a hack chaise' sits next to him Darcy maintains an offensive silence for a full thirty minutes. It is not surprising, then, that he bridles at the sociable Bingley's attempts to make him join in the dancing. . . .

Darcy's Class Prejudice

Because Darcy's attitude to her society is no better than it was when he rejected Bingley's similar proposal at the Meryton ball, Elizabeth is quite justified in refusing him. . . . Elizabeth, on the other hand, takes the view that because of his pride, the aristocrat is inevitably offensive in his dealings with those he considers to be his inferiors: 'I could easily forgive *his* pride, if he had not mortified *mine*.' The Darcys created by Charlotte and Elizabeth bear more resemblance to the actual man than young Lucas' Squire-Westernish aristocrat, who 'keep[s] a pack of foxhounds, and drink[s] a bottle of wine every day.' Nevertheless, all three are essentially stereotypes, based on preconceived notions rather than on any observation of actual conduct and as such are static figures incapable of moral growth. . . .

Elizabeth and Darcy have quickly developed an extremely frustrating relationship. He is attracted to her, but because he fails to go beyond stereotypes in approaching her milieu, and because of a combination of genuine objections to his behaviour and a similar weakness in her attitude to the aristocracy, there seems little chance that she will accept his advances. . . .

Darcy in Contrast to Bingley

In that Darcy's attitude to her family and its middle-class associations has still not improved, Elizabeth is justified in rejecting his approach once again. It would, after all, be hard to expect her to be receptive to a man who just previously had commented that the possession of relatives in Cheapside 'must very materially lessen their [Jane and Elizabeth's] chance of marrying men of any consideration in the world,' especially as his words contrast so unfavourably with Bingley's generous comment that 'if they had uncles enough to fill *all* Cheapside . . . it would not make them one jot less agreeable.' . . .

The Rude Aristocrat

Justifiable disapproval and prejudice alone, however, do not provide a sufficient explanation for the particularly virulent style in which Elizabeth rebuffs Darcy. She had just as much reason to think badly of him at Sir William Lucas' party, and yet she turned him down politely on that occasion: 'Indeed, Sir, I have not the least intention of dancing.—I entreat you not to suppose that I moved this way in order to beg for a partner.' Moreover, Elizabeth is never overtly rude to Lady Catherine de Bourgh, although she fits the aristocratic stereo-

Jennifer Ehle (as Elizabeth) and Colin Firth (as Darcy) promote the 1995 BBC TV production of Pride and Prejudice. *Darcy and Elizabeth's courtship in* Pride and Prejudice *is heavily influenced by class distinctions.* © Pictorial Press Ltd/Alamy.

type much better than Darcy and offers considerable provocation. Even the most outrageous of Lady Catherine's comments evoke nothing more than an amused or ironic response from Elizabeth. . . .

Darcy's rude treatment of Mrs Bennet during her visit only a few hours earlier justifies Elizabeth's continued disapproval. However, it becomes increasingly evident in the course of the day that her definition of him as an utter snob is inadequate, and that by clinging to it so rigidly she is depriving herself of opportunities to achieve a richer understanding of his character. The impropriety of Mrs Bennet's behaviour, for example, is a source of great embarrassment to Elizabeth herself: 'Darcy only smiled; and the general pause which ensued made Elizabeth tremble lest her mother should be exposing herself again.' Yet, she will not allow the possibility that Darcy's rudeness may have been caused by disapproval of Mrs Bennet's actual conduct as well as by objections to her low origins. . . .

Inherited Wealth

Although Bingley, who 'inherited property to the amount of nearly an hundred thousand pounds from his father,' is much wealthier than Jane, he does not regard himself as her social superior. His background is in trade, and he has not yet acquired the essential qualification of the gentleman—ownership of land. The Bennets, on the other hand, are a long-established family in possession of an estate, albeit entailed. There is, then, much to be gained on both sides from a match between a rising man of fortune and the daughter of a rather faded gentleman. Since Bingley and Jane are social equals, it is illogical that Darcy should be willing to associate with the Bingleys, but not with the Bennets. In the one case he quite properly balances off wealth and acquired gentility against low origins; in the other he perversely focuses almost entirely on the middle-class element introduced through marriage. This is perhaps because he finds it easier to accommodate himself to the faults of the Bingley family, which derive mainly from the aristocratic posturings of Caroline Bingley and Mrs Hurst, than to the unaccustomed vulgarity of some members of the Bennet family. Elizabeth is no less perverse since, in spite of

63

his sisters' aristocratic leanings, she accepts Bingley into her social universe, and yet she places his friend Darcy beyond the pale.

Learning About the Aristocracy

Some education is needed in order that Darcy and Elizabeth might come to recognise society as a network of interconnections broad enough to embrace Darcys, Bingleys and Bennets, and thereby clear the way for personal reconciliation. This is provided by visits to the aristocratic worlds of Rosings and Pemberley. Life at Rosings under Lady Catherine de Bourgh confirms Elizabeth's stereotypes, but Pemberley calls them into question, and compels her to arrive at a more complex and favourable view of the aristocracy. Darcy's perspective is broadened in a similar way. . . .

Union of the Classes

This union of aristocracy and gentry-middle class is not achieved easily; but it is possible, Jane Austen claims, because, despite their different social roles, the two groups are united by a shared ideal of concern for others. As Elizabeth tells Lady Catherine: 'In marrying your nephew, I should not consider myself as quitting that sphere. He is a gentleman; I am a gentleman's daughter; so far we are equal.' The moral strength of Pemberley, then, is not based so much on the exclusion of disruptive forces, although Lydia and Wickham are banned, but on the inclusion of responsible people from the aristocracy, the gentry and the middle class. Darcy and Elizabeth are resident, Bingley and Jane live close by, and the Gardiners from Gracechurch Street are the most welcome of visitors: 'With the Gardiners, they were always on the most intimate terms. Darcy, as well as Elizabeth, really loved them.'

Morality and Social Distinctions

John McAleer

John McAleer was professor of English at Boston College and author of Rex Stout: A Majesty's Life *(2002).*

The characters in Pride and Prejudice *represent various particular social positions, and their interactions are based on distinctions and exclusions. Darcy's moral growth is measured in his attitude toward the Gardiners, Elizabeth's aunt and uncle who run a business and live in the business district. Initially, when he is at his most arrogant and egotistical, and when Elizabeth dislikes him most intensely, Darcy is scornful of her relatives. When he later loses his extreme egotism in his love for Elizabeth, he welcomes the Gardiners into his life. McAleer argues that Jane Austen, whose family had respectability, if not money, was not in the least interested in reforming the rigid and exclusionary class system of her day, even though she parodies their foibles. Instead, McAleer shows that Austen believes that levels of moral behavior are reinforced by the traditional class system. What is to be repudiated is not the system but the individuals in the ranks of society who have dispensed with the high morals expected of their rank.*

The theme of disinheritance loomed large in Jane Austen's thoughts. Some critics see it as the axis her world rotates on. She took umbrage, too, at those who, swollen with pride of rank, treated their social inferiors meanly. Yet she did not call for the overthrow of a system of values and behaviour that had been the underpinning of civilization for centuries. Instead, she brought cool logic to bear on the problem. The social hierarchy, she concluded, as ideally constructed, is the outward manifestation of a moral hierarchy. It is this moral hierarchy that endows it with meaning and purpose. Ignore it and the social hierarchy becomes a sham apparatus devoid of function. In the country estate she saw this society emblemized. Administered by a caring landholder, a country estate was an embodiment of the natural moral order. Neglected, chaos enveloped it. She asked only that men would so conduct themselves that their behaviour would affirm the existence of a stable order energized by sound moral principles. This argument she expounds in *Pride and Prejudice* with care and thoroughness.

The Soldier Class

We begin with George Wickham. Without knowing his offence, Caroline Bingley dismisses him because he is the son of Darcy's father's steward: "considering his descent, one could not expect much better." This argument Elizabeth rejects. Wickham is a Cambridge graduate. His manners are perfect. She is responsive, however, when Mrs. Gardiner cautions her against the imprudence of encouraging such an attachment. Here, not prejudice but common sense is speaking. At issue is not Wickham's social position but his want of fortune. Later, however, when she [Elizabeth] declares, "Brother-in-law of Wickham! Every kind of pride must revolt from the connection," neither his [Wickham's] social standing nor his economic circumstances account for her revulsion. He is repudiated because he is unprincipled. For that reason alone he can never be received at Pemberley. Possibly he behaves as he does because he resents his social inferiority to Darcy, but the choice is his. Morally he is bankrupt.

Pride and Prejudice's second soldier is Darcy's cousin, Colonel Fitzwilliam. His place in the social hierarchy points to a flaw in that structure. He is the younger son of an earl. Though attracted to Elizabeth he is not at liberty to woo her.

Younger sons of noblemen were not free to follow their own hearts. He explains: "there are not many in my rank of life who can afford to marry without some attention to money." To marry for money was crass; to marry without it was folly. To find a compatible mate while keeping within this narrow corridor was no simple feat. Jane Austen spoke from personal knowledge. Yet it was one of the conditions which society, to maintain stability and order, necessarily imposed.

Class Mobility

The Bingleys, as a family, are passing from the middle class into the gentry. Predictably they exhibit the uneasiness such a transition involves. Their father has grown rich in trade and has educated his children to prepare them for social elevation. But to his son has fallen the task of acquiring a landed estate, the essential move that will establish him as a gentleman. For Bingley himself this step need impose no great difficulties. He is "gentlemanlike" and possesses "perfect good breeding." Mindful of Bingley's origins, Darcy concedes that it would not be socially damaging for him to marry Jane: "the want of connection could not be so great an evil to my friend as to me." But if Bingley is socially unambitious, his sisters are not. Elizabeth shows she has taken their measure when she says: "they may wish his increase of wealth and consequence; they may wish him to marry a girl who has all the importance of money, great connections, and pride." In her portrayal of Bingley's sisters, Jane Austen further develops her argument that no amount of money or manners makes sufficient amends when character is lacking. . . .

Prime focus centres on Caroline [Bingley]. Jane Nardin sums her up: "a social climber who values herself on the eloquence and fashion of her own behavior, which, however, is often contemptuous and rude." In attributing to Elizabeth "an abominable sort of conceited independence, a most country town indifference to decorum" and sneering at her muddy petticoats (one imagines after her sister's comment) and "blowsy" hair (a term the eighteenth century applied to beggars' trulls), she thinks to elevate herself above her, just as earlier she had taken pains to put distance between herself and Meryton community. . . Repudiating them, Jane Austen repudiates not the gentry but those who aspire to gentry status mistaking posturings of superiority for the essentials of character.

The Lucases [neighbors of the Bennets, Elizabeth's family], like the Bingleys, are caught in the act of slipping into the gentry, accompanied by a fortune garnered in trade. Although Caroline Bingley's self-importance entertains us, resentment tempers our amusement. The social aspirations of the Lucases also amuse us but occasion no resentment, only pity. Their aspirations rest on slight credentials. As mayor of Meryton, William Lucas spoke before the king and got a knighthood. Feeling the distinction perhaps "too strongly," he withdrew from business and set up as a landed gentleman at "Lucas Lodge" "where he could think with pleasure of his own importance." Sir William is not well enough circumstanced to launch his children successfully in their new life. His son's idea of being a gentleman is being able to "keep a pack of foxhounds, and drink a bottle of wine every day." His daughter's hopes centre on an establishment of her own, no matter that the man she settles for is a fool. Sir William appears ridiculous, mouthing platitudes and storing up noble names to drop in conversation. Through the Bingleys, Jane Austen satirizes those who must hold their inferiors in contempt to think well of themselves. Through the Lucases she satirizes those who must hold their superiors in awe to think well of themselves. Through neither does Jane Austen derogate the aristocracy. As interlopers they do discredit only to themselves.

Among those in *Pride and Prejudice* who are upwardly mobile, Mr. Collins stands supreme. Despite his kinship to Mr. Bennet [Mr. Collins is Mr. Bennet's nephew], he is of middle-class origins, and superior society is still a novelty to him. In social situations he is often at a loss. On meeting Mrs. Bennet's sister, the vulgar Mrs. Phillips, he protests "that except Lady Catherine and her daughter, he had never seen a more elegant woman." Part of the fun of this encounter is that Mrs. Phillips is equally awed by his seeming consequence. His misuse of the word "elegant," says [Norman] Page, "constitutes a damaging criticism of Mr. Collins and his standards." His presumption in forcing his acquaintance on Darcy further attests to his ignorance of the prevailing properties, a lamentable deficiency in one with his social ambitions.

Grateful to Lady Catherine for whatever crumbs she throws to him from her table, Mr. Collins schemes constantly to compliment her. . . . Undoubtedly he thinks that in marrying Charlotte Lucas, the daughter of a knight, he has enormously advantaged himself. Yet it is sad to learn that, apart from their evenings with Lady Catherine, when he must sound unceasing hosannahs in her praise, "Their other engagements were few; as the style of living of the neighborhood in general, was beyond the Collinses' reach." His life as a member of the gentry is a life of pretext, a fact he may never discover.

Class and Morality

Each character in *Pride and Prejudice* adds to our knowledge of the workings of the social hierarchy. Mrs. Bennet is no exception. By her marriage she has left the middle class. By her conduct she has stayed there. Habitually she finds herself on the defensive. Though Mr. Collins displays his own ignorance by assuming the Bennet girls have cooked dinner, Mrs. Bennet in the vehemence she shows in disabusing him, markedly overreacts. The only society the Bennets know is the Meryton society Mrs. Bennet sprang from. Presumably her vulgarity has been a bar to their acceptance by superior people. Her notion of what constitutes superior behaviour is simplistic, as when she says of Sir William, "He has always something to say to everybody—*That* is my idea of good breeding." What Darcy refers to as her "total want of propriety," is well illustrated by her indiscreet chatter. To her, social eminence has nothing to do with morals or manners. It is money and show. She translates the news of Elizabeth's engagement at once into material terms, as though to grasp it: "What pin-money, what jewels, what carriages you will have! . . . A house in town! . . . Ten thousand a year!" Then comes a further declaration: "You must and shall be married by a special license." Special licenses, by which marriages could be celebrated elsewhere than in the parish church, could be issued only by the archbishop and were costly. Hence their value as a status symbol.

The Gardiners as Moral Measure

The Gardiners are the source of an insight essential to our understanding of Jane Austen's sense of class structure. Mr. Gardiner is Mrs. Bennet's brother. He is in trade and lives within view of his own warehouses. Yet he is university educated and both he and his wife are well-bred. Sight unseen the Bingleys [sisters Caroline and Mrs. Hurst] put them down for "vulgar relations," and Darcy concludes that, for the Bennet sisters, having such an uncle "must very materially lessen their chance of marrying men of any consideration in the world." When Elizabeth first sees Pemberley she consoles herself by reflecting that, had she accepted Darcy, "my uncle and aunt would have been lost to me: I should not have been allowed to invite them." When the Gardiners are presented to Darcy (and here Elizabeth shows her good breeding by letting Darcy initiate the introduction), matters take a happy turn: "That he was *surprised* by the connexion was evident; he sustained it however with fortitude." What follows is a definite turning point in the novel. No longer are we dealing with people who are bidding for recognition or claiming a distinction they do not merit. The Gardiners are innately genteel. Darcy enters into conversation with Mr. Gardiner: "Elizabeth could not but be pleased, could not but triumph. It was consoling, that he should know she had some relations for whom there was no need to blush. She . . . gloried in every expression, every sentence of her uncle, which marked his intelligence, his taste, or his good manners." Darcy's acceptance of Mr. Gardiner affirms the pre-eminence of the moral hierarchy, which encompasses them both, over the arbitrary social hierarchy which hitherto has separated them. And so the way is open for him to come to Elizabeth on the same terms. Their perception of one another's moral worth makes all else incidental.

A Lack of Moral Wholeness

That Lady Catherine is to the manner and the matter born admits of no doubt. Through her, however, Jane Austen shows that improper pride of rank can be fully as objectionable as social presumptuousness, and may well be the greater offense since to dominate inferiors is an abuse of power. Lady Catherine uses her eminence to browbeat others. Even Darcy is, at times, appalled at her ill-breeding. Her brusqueness is never more marked than when she informs Elizabeth that she is unfit to be Darcy's wife:

> My daughter and my nephew are formed for each other. They are descended on the maternal side, from the same noble line; and, on the fathers,' from respectable, honourable, and ancient, though untitled families . . . and what is to divide them? The upstart pretensions of a young woman without family, connections, or fortune. . . . If you were sensible of your own good, you would not wish to quit the sphere, in which you have been brought up.

Parrying, now, Elizabeth's reply that her father is a gentleman, Lady Catherine rejoins, "But who was your mother? Who are your uncles and aunts? Do you imagine me ignorant of their conditions?"

By failing to judge others by their inherent worth, Lady Catherine shows she lacks that moral wholeness she must have to express the essence of the social hierarchy which she thinks she so perfectly embodies.

Darcy's pride of station and disdain for those of lesser distinction are factors paramount in any consideration of Jane Austen's sense of social hierarchy as set forth in [according to Mark Schorer] "a novel that founds its action on class barriers." Even Elizabeth's assertive individualism shows itself in its fullness only in reaction to Darcy's dismissive pride. Actually a measure of proper pride is Darcy's by entitlement. As Charlotte Lucas explains: "with family, fortune, every thing in his favour . . . he has a *right* to be proud." Further exculpation comes in his own account of the sense of exclusivity his parents had fostered in him:

> I have been a selfish being all my life, in practice, though not in principle. . . . I was given good principles but left to follow them in pride and conceit . . . allowed, encouraged, almost taught . . . to be selfish and overbearing, to care for none beyond my own family circle, to think meanly of the rest of the world, to *wish* at least to think meanly of their sense and worth compared with my own.

By telling Darcy that he has not conducted himself as a gentleman, Elizabeth opens his eyes to his moral failings. So complete is the reformation that follows, his love for Elizabeth survives even the gross immorality of Lydia's elopement. For her part, Elizabeth learns, from Darcy's caring behaviour, evident at Pemberley and extended now to the Gardiners and herself, that a sense of social identity is preferable to individualism.

As a voice heard from an obscure village, faulting society for entrenching itself behind a code it observed only in externals, Jane Austen might have been accounted a malcontent. She was nothing of the sort and gave no one occasion for thinking otherwise. She neither flailed the mighty nor celebrated their foes. In times past her family had renown beyond most men's dreams and she knew she was happier for its passing. What she did want was to see society re-embrace those principles which had been its traditional support, and she wrote to that end, sweeping away, in a surge of laughter, grievances that could not have been scoured away by an ocean of tears.

Money, Class, and Marriage

Edward Copeland

Edward Copeland, the F.S. Jennings Professor of English at Pomona College, is author of Women Writing About Money: Women's Fiction in England, 1790-1820 *(1995).*

Money in Pride and Prejudice *is used to buy, one's way, or marry one's way, to a higher social rank. Among the great social changes that occurred as a result of the Industrial Revolution was that many people became wealthy. The revolution in agriculture put money in the hands of those who possessed significant acres of land. Inflation and economic depression made the securing of capital an absolute imperative, and marriage became a means to this end. Edward Copeland contends that Austen is mainly concerned with the economic situation of her own class. He provides comparative figures with which to imagine the lifestyle of various classes. A hardworking maid was paid twenty-five pounds a year, scarcely enough to live on. In contrast, Elizabeth's father had 2,000 pounds a year, enough to keep a horse and some household help. Mr. Darcy, who has both class status and money, had 10,000 pounds a year.*

Money in Jane Austen's novels has an uncanny way of seeming so much like our own that we run the serious mistake of thinking that it is. Everything in the Austen novels seems to add up at the cash register in the usual way—the pianos, shawls, muslins, carriages and horses—so familiar that we think we are in the same world. We are not. The Austen fictional economy draws on a real economy in a state of rapid and unsettling transition: an expanding commercial sector, a rapidly developing consumer culture, an economy tied to the

Edward Copeland, *Jane Austen in Context*. New York: Cambridge University Press, 2005. Copyright © 2005 Cambridge University Press. Reprinted with the permission of Cambridge University Press.

ups and downs of foreign wars, high taxes, scarce capital, inadequate banking and credit systems and large sums of money to be made and spent by those who never had it before. Aggressive enclosures of common lands, consolidation of neighbouring farms and the introduction of modern agricultural improvements had brought enormous wealth and power to the great landholders. These conspicuous and deeply felt changes in the distribution and management of wealth were made even more acute by an unheard of rate of inflation in prices, punctuated by periodic economic depression. In this unstable economy, marriage, Austen's narrative mainstay, was a legitimate and common means of gaining access to all-important capital.

Financial Trouble

People without money, or living on fixed incomes, or tied to older patriarchal systems of financial support were in big trouble, or so it seemed in the 1790s when Austen's first three novels, *Sense and Sensibility* (1795, 1797), *Pride and Prejudice* (1796–7) and *Northanger Abbey* (1798–9), were conceived. These early novels share a common economic vision—the danger of losing it all, the chance of hitting it rich, huge losses, huge gains, everything riding on luck and the main chance. . . .

Jane Austen's Interest in the Economy

Jane Austen's interest in the economy appears in her earliest works, possibly when she was only thirteen years of age, in 'Edgar and Emma,' for example, which parodies the vague economic clichés of sentimental novels by introducing 'Mr. Willmot of Willmot Lodge . . . the representative of a very ancient Family & possessed besides his paternal Estate, a considerable share in a Lead mine & a ticket in the Lottery.' Money comes into view in Austen's novels, however, mainly through the focussing lens of her own social rank. This group of genteel professionals, situated in the country and consisting of clergymen of the Anglican church, men in the law (preferably barristers), officers in the army and navy and rentiers retired from business and of large fortune, has been called by the historian David Spring the 'pseudo-gentry,' a mischievous but sharp description of the group's social position. They were, writes Spring, 'gentry of a sort, primarily because they sought strenuously to be taken for gentry.' Sandwiched between commerce and the landed gentry, the pseudo-gentry made use of consumer goods to assert their claims to social consequence. Consumer power drove the value of that negotiable concept of an income that contemporaries called the 'competence.'

[Scottish philosopher and economist] Adam Smith defined the term competence in its broadest social inclusion, that is, 'whatever the custom of the country renders it indecent for creditable people, even of the lowest order, to be without.' But, as John Trusler, a contemporary economist, writes in his *Domestic Management*, 'What is competency to one, is not so to another.' As he explains: 'Wealth is comparative: that which would make one man rich, another shall be poor with. Every man should be able to live, and make an appearance in life, equal to his station in it.' . . .

Comparison of Incomes

As a comparison, a common labourer at the lowest end of the economic scale would earn around £25 a year, including extra work during harvests, a sum, according to [British author] Anna Laetitia Barbauld, on which he was expected to maintain 'himself, his wife, and half a dozen children in food, lodging, clothes, and fuel.' [British author] Hannah More provides an idea of the family's diet in the recipe she recommends for them in her *Cheap Repository Tracts*: in a mess of garden vegetables supplemented with 'a bit of coarse beef, a sheep's head, or any such thing,' with the meat to go to the father, the working man; 'the children don't want it,' she says cheerfully,

Historically, enlisting in the military gave middle and lower class men an opportunity to rise in social rank. Women rose in rank through marriage. © Visual Arts Library (London)/Alamy.

'the soup will be thick and substantial, and requires no bread.' [British author] Mary Wollstonecraft wrote to her sister of a governess's position available at £25 per annum, a situation that would provide food and shelter, but not enough money, as she knew from her own experience, to cover the cost of appropriate dress for the parlour. Up a step, at £40 a year, a curate with a house and garden would have almost twice the income, but also the duty of appearing like a gentleman. As Anne Plumptre explains in *The Rector's Son*, 'Placed in a situation in which they are expected to sustain the rank of gentlemen, they have scarcely the means of procuring even the common necessaries of life, much less of obtaining those superfluities which are considered as essential appendages to that of rank.' Austen's published works seldom reach this far down the scale in consumer distress. . . .

Landed estates, however, provide the most prominent unit for measuring competences in Austen's novels: Mr Bennet, for example, has an estate worth £2,000 per annum, Mr Darcy, £10,000 per annum. An heiress's fortune, in contrast, is given as a lump sum figure, which then must be calculated for the annual income it yields, the presumption being that it is invested in the government funds at an annual interest rate of 5 per cent. This holds true in all of Austen's novels, with an exception in *Pride and Prejudice*, where the question arises of a choice between 4 or 5 per cent. Mrs Bennet, who, if she does not understand entails [refers to the legal practice of keeping property from descending to a female relative—in this case, on Mr. Bennet's death, the Bennet estate is to go to his nephew, Mr. Collins, instead of to one of his five daughters], does understand incomes, is scrupulous in reporting Mr Bingley's potential income, using both 4 and 5 per cent multipliers to convert his known inheritance of £100,000 into its annual income from investment in the funds: 'A single man of large fortune,' she tells Mr Bennet, 'four or five thousand a year. What a fine thing for our girls!' . . .

How Far Did Money Go?

The great question for modern readers of Austen's novels, however, concerns the consumer power of these incomes. The effort to understand the power of incomes is not idle speculation, either in Austen's time or now. Contemporaries were actively interested in knowing the incomes of their neighbours, which were scarcely private since the values of clerical livings, landed estates and great inheritances were publicly known, but also because the topic itself was not hedged with the secrecy it possesses today. Letters and diaries sent along the news of other peoples' incomes almost as a duty. Susan Ferrier, for example, reports that her friend Anne Walker has told her that Mr Knatchbull, the groom in a recent match, 'is very handsome, and has 500 *l.* a year, so for a poor *plainish* miss it is no bad match.' Jane Austen confides to Cassandra information of the same kind about their brother: 'Frank limits himself, I believe, to four hundred a year.' With the instability that an expanding consumer economy inevitably brings to hierarchies of rank, it was essential to evaluate and to fix, if possible, acceptable relationships between incomes, rank and spending practices.

The lowest competence alluded to in Austen's novels is an income of £100 a year. On this amount a *'widow* or other *unmarried Lady,* may keep a *Young Maid Servant,* and a low salary; say from 5 to 10 Guineas a year,' according to Samuel and Sarah Adams in their domestic guide *The Complete Servant.* . . . When Mrs Jennings in *Sense and Sensibility* believes that Lucy and Edward are to marry on only £100 a year, she takes immediate pity on them: 'I must see what I can give them towards furnishing their house. Two maids and two men indeed!—as I talked of t'other day.—No, no, they must get a stout girl of all works.'

For Austen, a competence of £300 a year is only slightly less marginal. In *Sense and Sensibility* this sum will make Edward Ferrars comfortable as a bachelor, says Colonel Brandon, but will not enable him to marry. 'The Colonel is a ninny,' says Mrs Jennings, who as a merchant's wife understands the lower range of competences better than Colonel Brandon. Mrs Jennings is certain, though mistakenly, that Lucy, the niece of a provincial schoolmaster, will be glad enough to marry on that sum. Elinor and Edward, Lucy's superiors in rank and in consumer expectations, are 'neither of them quite enough in love to think that three hundred and fifty pounds a year would supply them with the comforts of life.' They postpone their marriage until better prospects arrive. James Austen, Jane's eldest brother who was married on £300 a year, quickly discovered that it would not support his ambitious notions of a competence: a close carriage for his wife and a pack of harriers for his hunting pleasures. . . .

A competence of £500 a year is greeted in most women's fiction as a thoroughly genteel income for a single woman.

The Adams' *Complete Servant* suggests that a widow with this competence could have three servants: two women and a boy, and an occasional gardener. . . .

At the highest income levels of the Austen family's professional rank, a competence of between £800 and £1,500 a year brings significant consumer signs along with it. Trusler suggests that £800 a year will support a carriage, though the Adamses suggest that the purchase would be more prudent for incomes between £1,000 and £1,500 a year. . . . Jane Austen's father set up a carriage when his income reached £700 a year, but soon gave it up as too expensive.

The largest incomes in Austen's novels are most frequently reserved for the landed gentry and are characterised by the degree and kind of consumer display undertaken by their possessors. . . . In *Pride and Prejudice* Mr Bennet's estate is worth £2,000 a year, which he just keeps within, though without making any provisions for dowries for his daughters. Mr Darcy's £10,000 a year from the Pemberley estate is spent admirably on furniture that has 'less of splendour, and more elegance, than the furniture of Rosings.' He also refurnishes a parlour solely for his sister's pleasure and makes a substantial contribution of resources for the sake of Elizabeth to retrieve Lydia's honour, such as it is.

The "Big Bow-Wow" of Social Change

Christopher Kent

Christopher Kent is a professor of history at the University of Saskatchewan, an editor of the Canadian Journal of History, *and the author of* Brains and Numbers: Elitism, Comtism, and Democracy in Mid-Victorian England *(1978).*

Jane Austen has been taken to task by some critics because she does not mention in her novels the great big "bow-wow" of her age, specifically the French Revolution and the Industrial Revolution, both of which turned the world, particularly ideas of class, upside down. Yet Christopher Kent maintains in this essay that she clearly takes into account the effects these events had on the lives of middle-class gentry. He argues that nowhere is her acknowledgement of the world at large so apparent than in her portraits of the militia in Pride and Prejudice. *The scoundrel Wickham is easily able to climb to the rank of officer in the militia, which is regarded as inferior to the regular army. Then he is able to secure a commission in the more highly regarded army with money provided by Darcy. Wickham's being shipped to the industrial North of England shows Austen's awareness of disruption among the working poor, who had been inspired by French ideas of social equality.*

To the social historian, the apparent preoccupation of literary critics with the historical dimensions of Jane Austen's canvas suggests limitations in their conception of history more than limitations in her art. It reflects a 'big bow-wow' view of history, to adapt Sir Walter Scott's phrase, in which certain epic events—the French Revolution, the Industrial Revolution—tower over all others. . . .

Christopher Kent, *Jane Austen in a Social Context*. Lanham, MD: Barnes & Noble Books, 1981. Copyright © 1981 Christopher Kent. All rights reserved. Reproduced by permission of Palgrave Macmillan.

The Historical Background

The novelist is in danger of being judged chiefly by the degree to which he fits retrospectively prescribed emphases and directions into the historical background of his work. Notoriously, Jane Austen fails these tests. Quite unashamedly she seems to flout Fanny Burney's Law: that it is 'impossible to delineate any picture of human life without reference to the French Revolution'. . . .

It can be argued that early nineteenth-century England was much more diverse, regionally, economically, socially and culturally than it is today, and that to talk of the 'real England' of that time, therefore, is even less admissible. . . .

The notion that Jane Austen's world is a bourgeois idyll belongs to this genre: it attempts to escape the problem of the author's mimetic intentions, and of the novel's specific temporal and physical reference by elevating her whole landscape into idea. . . .

There can be no doubt that the popular image of nineteenth-century England owes far more to Austen, [Charles] Dickens and [John] Galsworthy than it does to historians. But is worth recalling that Jane Austen did not regard herself as an historian of her society in the way, for instance, that [George] Eliot, [George] Meredith or [Thomas] Hardy did. This gives her novels a peculiar interest and value to the historian as historical evidence, as historical documents, precisely because they are not self-consciously 'historical'. Because she has not tried to do the historian's work, to mediate and shape her world into something recognisably historical, she deserves the historian's attention and respect. . . .

This is not to suggest that Jane Austen was unaware of history. Quite the opposite. Her decision not to write history was a conscious one; not to write history as she understood it, not 'real, solemn history'. It is evident that she was much interested in history from a very early age, witness her precocious 'History of England' (1791), a hilarious and quite sophisticated parody of 'partial [and], prejudiced' historians whose history was chiefly a vehicle for their social and political beliefs. She caricatures a number of errors which, in less blatant form, have been committed by very eminent historians. . . .

The Officer Class

All this may seem rather a weight of history to place on a few slender passages from Jane Austen's novels, but of course the point is that the novels are not *about* the Industrial Revolution: only that being realistic representations from the time and place of the Industrial Revolution, they cannot avoid it, and it is in fact right where it should be. But what of the French Revolution? 'It never occurred to Jane Austen', writes Harry Levin, 'that the young officers who figure as dancing partners for the heroines of her novels were on furlough from Trafalgar and Waterloo'. This breathtaking assertion of ignorance and condescension hardly deserves refutation, since the most cursory reading of *Persuasion* alone, even of its last paragraph, explodes the suggestion that Jane Austen was ignorant of the navy's military, as opposed to its social, role. But while much has been written about the importance of the navy in her novels—and her life—less attention has been given to the army, concerning which Levin's remark might be taken by some to be at least not quite so wrongheaded.

The army figures prominently only in *Pride and Prejudice*, though characters in the other novels are significantly connected with it. For instance, Jane Fairfax is an orphan because her father, a soldier, died in action. Colonel Brandon, a gentry younger son, went off to serve in India to forget a thwarted love affair, and, though generally felt to be rather a stick, adheres to the military code of honour to the extent of fighting in the only duel mentioned in the novels. But the army as it figures in *Pride and Prejudice* is not the regular army; it is significantly the militia. This was a highly localised and rather amateur body raised solely for the defence of Great Britain. There were indeed riots in 1796 when it was suggested by the government that the militia might be forced to serve abroad, even in Ireland. So far was it from being 'on furlough from Waterloo'. With its purely defensive role the militia was particularly visible in the South of England because of French invasion threats from across the Channel. And because it had considerable leisure, awaiting an invasion that never came, it is not surprising that this army appeared to Mrs Bennet and her younger daughters chiefly as an incentive to visit the local lending library (apparently a popular meeting place), an agency of dances and a market for husbands. Such a consumer view was quite appropriate in the circumstances. It is appropriate also that Mr Wickham, a militia officer, should be the major disruptive force in the plot since the militia was itself a somewhat irregular and, potentially at least, radical organisation, being an eighteenth-century English version of the citizen army. It was originally intended as a sort of counterpoise to the regular standing army of the king. Because militia commissions were not purchased, it was much less exclusive than the regular army and consequently lacked the latter's social prestige. The militia had difficulty in attracting suitable officers however, which explains the presence of George Wickham, ne'er do well son of an estate steward. However, Wickham ends up in the regular army, thanks to Darcy's paying his debts and buying him a commission. Such is the rather precarious regularisation of Wickham and his marriage in the new social equilibrium established at the novel's end.

The Battle Between Social Classes

Even as a regular soldier, Wickham is not sent abroad, but to Newcastle in the turbulent industrial North. This recalls another point: that the army was not simply for use against foreign enemies. In the almost complete absence of effective police forces in England the army was central to the maintenance

of public order at home. Thus, while war raged on the conti-
nent considerable detachments of regulars had to be kept at
home for use particularly in the frequently troubled industrial
areas, for the years of the French Revolution were of course
years of great political and social unrest in England. Even in
rural Hampshire Jane Austen was aware of this; her brothers
after all served in the navy, which suffered serious mutinies in
1797 which were widely thought to be inspired by Jacobin
agitators. . . .

The Avoidance of Revolution

To conclude, the reader of Jane Austen should listen not so
much for history's 'big bow-wow', but, following the advice of
Sherlock Holmes, listen for the dog that did not bark. If the
French Revolution does not loom so visibly in her novels as it
does in the history texts, one should perhaps reflect on the
significance of that absence. The great French historian Elie
Halévy, his ears accustomed to the din of revolution in the
history of his own country, did a great service to the study of
English history when he seriously addressed the question of
why England escaped revolution at the turn of the nineteenth
century. The answer he suggested was that the religious re-
vival, and particularly the Methodist movement, generated a
sort of antibody to revolution in the English body politic.
There has since been considerable debate over the 'Halévy
Thesis', and social historians, as they refine their techniques
for recovering the largely undocumented lives, attitudes and
activities of the ordinary people, will be able to come closer to
answering such questions. Although social historians are cur-
rently somewhat preoccupied with the working classes, it is
perhaps to the 'middling classes', Jane Austen's own province,
that one should look for an answer to Halévy's question. They
emerge from her novels as a confident group who could in-
souciantly borrow a dance from the French Revolution (the
Boulanger) and dance it at the Meryton Assembly, who had

strength of nerve in their economic endeavours and faith in their own values and standards. They were by no means a homogeneous stratum, as the contemporary phrase 'middling classes' suggests; indeed, their relative fluidity was ultimately a source of social stability in that it left fewer opportunities for the dangerous accumulation of social frustrations. Read from this point of view Jane Austen's novels are not about history, not self-conscious substitutes for, or rivals to it. They are themselves the very evidence of social history.

Changes in Class Structure and Values

Terry Eagleton

Professor of cultural theory and John Rylands Fellow at the University of Manchester, Terry Eagleton is the author of Sweet Violence: The Idea of the Tragic *(2003) and* Literary Theory: An Introduction *(1983).*

Terry Eagleton's view is that Jane Austen, who grew up and wrote in a time of social turbulence, parodied the misbehavior of members of her own rank and those above her but was not considered to be a social liberal or reformer. Austen saw the polite manners and propriety of genteel society as a positive civilizing influence on the working class and the nouveau riche as a whole. While Austen supports the system of rank within British society, believing that its form and order are the nation's moral base, the "moral rot" of the genteel classes started with their growing materialism, crass capitalism, and view of land as investment property rather than soil intended to be tilled. Austen's intent was not to recommend an upheaval of the social system but to show the way back to the traditional, moral leadership once held by the gentry before the rise of crass commercialism, the importance of wealth, and the increase in social mobility.

That this period [the late eighteenth and early nineteenth centuries] should have witnessed such an extraordinary burst of novelistic experiment is hardly surprising. It was, after all, an epoch of dramatic social and political upheaval: revolution in France and North America, the Napoleonic conquests, the massive expansion of empire, Britain's dominance of the seas, the prosperity reaped from the slave trade, the rise

Terry Eagleton, *The English Novel*. Oxford, UK: Blackwell Publishing, 2005. Copyright © 2005 by Terry Eagleton. All rights reserved. Reproduced by permission of Blackwell Publishers.

of the European nation-state, the increasing capitalist 'rationalization' of the countryside as common rights were uprooted by so-called enclosures. The period saw the beginnings of the industrial revolution, the consolidation of middle-class power, and the first stirrings of the organized, politically vocal working class. It was a time of radical movements and ideas, which found themselves confronting what in the heyday of [Sir Walter] Scott and [Jane] Austen was effectively a British police state. The new experiments in fiction had some of their roots in this era of vision and anxiety, in new liberations of energy and new forms of repression. . . .

Parodying Her Own Class

Irony of Austen's kind is clearly different from the scabrous, virulent satire of a[n] [Alexander] Pope or [Jonathan] Swift— though like them she is concerned to defend a traditional way of life against outside interlopers and inside subversives. Her tone is less bluff and breezy than [Henry] Fielding's, her irony more subtle but also on the whole less genial. It is the tone of one who is criticizing from the inside, constrained by the proprieties of the very social set-up she is taking to task, but also by the fact that the targets of her satire are for the most part her own kind. Or rather she is, like so many of the novelists who came after her, inside and outside at the same time, and the nature of her irony, which is reproving but not abrasive, reflects this ambiguity.

Austen was the daughter of a clergyman of limited financial means, finished her formal education at the age of nine, and earned £1000 at most from her writing. Her family, however, had a number of connections with the wealthier gentry. She hailed, then, from a subaltern section of the gentry, one which identified strongly with that class's values and traditions but found itself exposed and insecure. She is no great admirer of the high aristocracy, as we can see from her portrait of the appalling Lady Catherine de Bourgh in *Pride and*

Prejudice. Such *grandes dames* and their overprivileged men-folk bring out her rebellious middle-class instincts. Rather as later nineteenth-century novelists find themselves marooned between the upper-middle class and the common people, so Austen lives out a similar conflict a few social notches higher, caught between patrician magnates and the middle classes. . . .

Propriety in the Genteel Class

Morally upright conduct is inseparable from respect, compassion and sensitivity, and thus from manners, civility or propriety in the true senses of those terms. Civility means not just not spitting in the sugar bowl, but not being boorish, arrogant, conceited, long-winded and insensitive. Propriety includes not just how to wield a fish knife, but, as the word suggests, a sense of what is proper to others and to oneself—of what is due, fit and proportionate, rather than mean, incongruous or grotesquely excessive. A more weighty word for what is fit, due and proper is 'just'. The idea of propriety is bound up with notions of prudence, considerateness and respect: it would be improper to leave a young woman alone with a young man in certain circumstances, since she might be vilely slandered as a result, and so might unjustly suffer. . . .

Morality and Training

As far as the moral life goes, Austen seems to believe in both innate dispositions and the importance of education. Some people just are naturally vain and selfish; but a lot of immoral behaviour in the novels flows from weak or irresponsible parenting, not least on the part of fathers. She rejects the sentimentalist delusion that morality is simply a question of doing what comes naturally—though she also seems to consider that when you *have* successfully disciplined and transformed yourself, you will find, like the two elder Bennet sisters [Jane and Elizabeth], that you do what is proper without needing to think too much about it. This is the right kind of instinctiveness, rather than, like Romantic impulse, the wrong one.

You need, then, to develop a spontaneous sense of what is morally appropriate—though it will not, to be sure, be an infallible one. . . .

The Moral Crisis in Social Upheaval

If morality matters so much to Jane Austen, it is partly because of an historical crisis. It is not a crisis which enters her novels directly; indeed, it is not one which Austen is aware of as such, though she was certainly conscious of its symptoms. Unlike Scott, she does not think in historical terms. It is a commonplace that her novels have few comments pass on the great social and political events of the day. Nobody asks where Louis Napoleon is in [Charles] Dickens, but plenty of people seem to ask where Napoleon Bonaparte is in Austen. In fact, Austen does allude to public events of the day. . . . In any case, as Raymond Williams points out in *The Country and the City*, Austen's novels concern the social history of the landed gentry, and it is hard to find a topic more central to English history than that. Jane Austen did not write about the family rather than society; on the contrary, the family in her day *was* society, or at least the governing sector of it. In the eighteenth century, a few hundred families owned a quarter of the cultivated land of England.

Failing Morality Among Gentry

Yet the class which these families composed was morally failing, and it is part of the business of Jane Austen's writing to recall it to its traditional sense of duty. Throughout the eighteenth century, the gentry had been a superbly self-confident class, one whose political dominance over English society as a whole went largely unquestioned. As Austen is writing, it is about to confront a formidable rival in the form of the urban middle class, which is being ushered over the historical horizon by the industrial revolution. But this is still largely in the future; and even when industrial capitalism has arrived on the scene, the landed gentry will come to strike an historic bargain with it. They will continue to exercise political and cultural power themselves, even if, as the nineteenth century wears on, they will find themselves governing increasingly in the name of their middle-class inferiors.

What concerns Austen is not so much these challenges from outside, but threats to the governing bloc of gentry and aristocracy from within. The English landed gentry was a capitalist class—in fact, it was the oldest capitalist class in the world. We are not dealing, then, with a case of 'traditional' versus 'modern'. On the contrary, it is precisely because the rural gentry had long been a 'modern' as well as a 'traditional' class, involved in rent, capital and property as well as in balls in Bath and ceremonies at court, that the moral rot had set in. Land had long been a commodity, and it is certainly that in Austen's fiction. She has a notably quick eye for the size and value of an estate, along with the likely social status of its proprietor. But she is not generally so entranced by an estate's physical and natural appearance, and we rarely see anyone working in its fields. 'Land' is more a monetary abstraction than an expanse of soil. It is seen as property, not as a working environment, as it is in Thomas Hardy. The English countryside had long since been reorganized by market forces. In Austen's own day it was living through a particularly devastating phase of that process, in the enclosure of land for the purpose of increased profits.

Responsibility of English Gentry

Yet the class of rural gentry to which Austen belonged—a class of which she is both an astringent critic and an ardent champion—did not quite see itself in these crudely economic terms. Even though it was investing more and more in overseas trade and the financial markets, it could still regard itself as a paternalist, traditionally minded squirearchy [class of landed gentry]. Its privileges, so it maintained, brought with them responsibility for the welfare of the lower orders. Hence the regulation trips to poor tenants' cottages and dutiful tendings of low-life sick beds which figure in Austen's writing. The gentry was not just a group of entrepreneurs but the apex of a whole rural way of life, one which was thought to embody the finest values of English society. Culture in the sense of the cultivation of the land—agriculture—generated rents, which in turn gave birth to culture in the sense of elegance of manners and nobility of spirit. In some ways, then, these landed aristocrats and country gentlemen continued to cultivate a traditional rural lifestyle, even if this cultural self-image was increasingly at odds with their economic base. It is this kind of rural order which Austen admired and upheld.

Social Mobility

Yet the business dealings of the gentry were in danger of corrupting their traditional values from within, as well as bringing them into closer contact with the tainting influences of commerce, finance and the city. And this, in Austen's eyes, was at risk of insidiously undermining their moral standing. She drew, then, on the cultivation which genteel society afforded her, in order to criticize something of the material base which made that cultivation possible. Social mobility, for example, was on the increase, which posed a threat to the rural tranquillity which Austen esteemed so highly. Urban wealth, restless social ambition, moral frivolity and metropolitan manners were infiltrating the countryside. They were doing so not least through the marriage market, as landed capital sought a new lease of life by assimilating through marriage the children of urban capitalists and financiers. . . .

It is the traditional English alliance between urban and agrarian capital, one which was later to be pursued in so-called public schools where the sons of both classes were able to rub shoulders. It played its part in securing for England an enviably resilient ruling class, one fit for its role in running an enormous empire.

Danger in Class Mobility

All this, however, seemed to more conservative gentry like Austen to be in dire danger of lowering the moral and cultural tone of English rural life. It was not just upstarts, blow-ins and social climbers like Mr Elton in *Pride and Prejudice* who were causing the trouble. . . .

Darcy in *Pride and Prejudice* is a rich land-owner of a venerable family who has inherited his estate, whereas his friend Bingley is looking to purchase an estate since he will not inherit one. Sir William Lucas in the same novel has risen from trade to a knighthood, while Mr Bennet has some landed wealth but has married into the professional middle classes. . . .

Jane Austen was by no means opposed in principle to trade or the professions. . . . Neither is there anything inherently shameful about urban or mercantile capitalism. The danger lies at the moral and cultural level, not at the material one. For it was on their culture, in the broad sense of values, standards, ideals and a fine quality of living, that the landowning classes had relied for so much of their authority. Their purpose had been to achieve hegemony—to win the loyalty and assent of their underlings by their moral example—rather than simply to rule them by force. And the English landed classes had been on the whole remarkably successful in this project. If this hegemony now started to crumble from within, in a society already shaken to its roots by riots, spy scares, agrarian discontent, economic depression, working-class militancy, the threat of revolution abroad and invasion at home, then the situation could scarcely be more serious.

Manners and Misrule

'Manners', wrote Edmund Burke, 'are more important than laws'. This, in a word, is the creed of the kind of gentry whom

Austen commends. It is by translating laws and codes into beguiling forms of behaviour that men and women come to appreciate their force. What secures the allegiance of the lower orders is not simply a set of abstract precepts from on high, but the graceful, well-ordered, socially responsible forms of a whole way of life. It is culture, nor [*sic*] coercion, which is the key to sound government. Indeed, what else is the realist novel but a way of translating abstractions into living characters and dramatic situations? As such, it is a small model of political hegemony in itself, winning our approval for its values not through abstract argument, but by transforming those values into lived experience. The common people may scarcely make a showing in Austen's novels, but they are bound to figure implicitly in any reflection on a decline in ruling-class standards. Not just the common people of England, either: if English upper-class 'character' is flawed and defective, how can one govern the empire?

Nothing could be more ominous, then, than a governing class which is plagued by moral misrule. The custodians of English culture have become infected by various forms of anarchy, from the disowning of parental authority to the giddy pursuit of fashion, from vulgar self-seeking to heartless economic calculation, from sexual flightiness to the worship of money. And Austen, as we have suggested, raises her voice to recall them to their true vocation. It is one of the limits of her vision, however, that she portrays the problem chiefly as a moral one, rather than grasping its historical and political roots. . . .

Codes and the Gentry

It is sometimes pointed out that the English have a deep-rooted tradition of moral thought, but not so well developed a heritage of political, sociological and philosophical ideas. Morality rather than sociology is the English forte, from Samuel Johnson to George Orwell. And this is one important reason why the novel has flourished so abundantly in England, since the novel can be seen as a supremely moral form. In fact, the evolution of the nineteenth-century realist novel is bound up with a sea-change in the very idea of morality—roughly speaking, from morality as a matter of timeless codes and absolute principles, to morality as a concern with qualities of lived experience.

In English culture, then, the moral has acted in one sense to displace social and political thought. This is evident enough in the fiction of Jane Austen, whom we admire among other things for her extraordinary moral intelligence. Only Henry James is her equal here. On the whole, the English have preferred to preach rather than to analyze, to attend to sins and solecisms rather than social structures. Yet moral values, as we have argued, were indeed vital to the continuing authority of the English upper classes—so that this preoccupation with morals and manners was not simply a displacement of more fundamental questions. Morals and manners were part of high politics. And since they were primarily the concern of women, women being stereotypically supposed to be specialists in such matters, this meant that so-called women's issues lay very close to the heart of the public sphere, even if they were rarely acknowledged to do so.

If one way in which women can help regenerate the gentry is by writing about it, another is by marrying into it. . . . Marriages in Austen do not need to involve material equality: a woman with a small marriage portion can marry a much grander man, as the elder Bennet sisters do. . . .

Love and Titles

A title and a spectacular fortune are of no value to you if you do not love their possessor. Indeed, few things are more morally appalling in Austen's world than marrying for social or financial gain. All the same, the fact that you should not make a fetish of wealth and status does not mean that you should cavalierly ignore them. . . .

When Elizabeth Bennet remarks that she first became aware of her affection for Darcy when she set eyes on his elegantly laid-out estates, we suspect for a moment that her author is being ironic, as though Elizabeth were to confide that she fell in love with him when she first clapped eyes on his bank balance. But the comment is not of course intended as ironic, since the material or external can and should be an outward sign of the inner or moral. The taste, sound judgement, sense of proportion, and blending of tact and imagination which went into the fashioning of Darcy's estates testify to a morally estimable character. It is not surprising in this light that Jane Austen should have remarked that she could imagine marrying the poet George Crabbe even though she had never met him. Ideally, there is a correlation between the moral and the material, of which marriage is the consummation. In choosing a marriage partner, both the inward or spiritual (love) and the external or material (rank, property, family) must be given due weight. Marriage is the union of the subjective and objective. It is the place where social forms and moral values most vitally intersect. . . .

Material impoverishment by no means entails moral impoverishment, just as social grandeur by no means entails moral magnificence. If it did, the word 'gentleman', which hovers ambiguously between a social and a moral sense, would be less of a fraught term in English social history than it is. . . .

A Social Conservative

The English have traditionally admired balance, symmetry, moderation and sound judgement, and there is plenty of these qualities in Austen. They are present not only in the values she speaks up for, but in the very formal design of her fiction itself. Form in Austen is already a moral position. Yet she is not, any more than Walter Scott, a devotee of the middle way. Sense is more trustworthy than sensibility; objectivity more precious than subjective feeling; deference, hierarchy and tradition more to be prized than dissidence or individual freedom. Like Scott, she is a 'modern' conservative rather than a Romantic reactionary, believing as she does in the need for reform and improvement within the status quo.

Distinctions Within the Circle of Family and Friends

Juliet McMaster

Juliet McMaster retired as professor emeritus at the University of Alberta, Edmonton. She is the author of Jane Austen the Novelist: Essays Past and Present *(1996) and* Thackeray: The Major Novels *(1971).*

Social ranks in England are intrinsic to most novels. This is particularly the case with the novels of Jane Austen. In her novels, however, the topmost rank of royalty is ignored, and titled aristocrats, such as "Sir" Lucas and Lady Catherine, are the objects of scorn. The prince in this Cinderella tale is Darcy, an untitled but wealthy man who, by virtue of his rank, is expected to be a man with a higher sense of morals and social responsibility. Juliet McMaster stresses the class distinctions within families. Sons have higher rank than daughters; the eldest son is ranked higher than the younger ones; eldest daughters are ranked above their younger sisters; and married daughters rank higher than unmarried ones. Austen also portrays the military class of soldiers made attractive by their uniforms to silly young girls. The rank of tradesmen, to the disgust of Lady Catherine, is gradually breaking class boundaries.

We hear of Lady Catherine de Bourgh, one of the most memorable and least likeable characters in Jane Austen's novels, that 'she likes to have the distinction of rank preserved'. The obsequious Mr. Collins enjoins her guest Elizabeth Bennet to dress simply, and not to emulate the elegant apparel of her high-ranking hostess: the differences in station are not only present, but must be *seen* to be present.

Class difference was of course a fact of life for Austen, and an acute observation of the fine distinctions between one social level and another was a necessary part of her business as a writer of realistic fiction. Nor would she have wished it away, although at the time of writing her novels, she herself—as the unmarried daughter of a deceased country clergyman, like Miss Bates—knew what it was to suffer from the class system. Her favourite niece, Fanny Knight, 'whom she had seen grow up from a period when her notice was an honour', was shamelessly patronizing after she married a lord, and said her aunt, but for the advantages she gained at Godmersham, would have been 'very much below par as to good Society and its ways'. . . .

Titled Aristocracy

Although in her own life Austen did have some dealings with royalty, however mediated, when she was graciously invited to dedicate *Emma* to the Prince Regent, she never presents royalty in her fiction, nor any of the great aristocrats who still owned great tracts of the country, and were prominent in its government. So we must start several rungs down the ladder. . . . So much suggests that for Austen there is nothing divine about royalty, and not much that is special about peers. In fact characters with titles—or 'handles to their names', as the Victorians used to say—are seldom admirable in the novels. . . .

A baronetcy is an inherited title, passed down from father to son; a knighthood, also signalled by the title 'Sir' attached to the first name, is awarded for a particular service; since it is not hereditary, it carries less prestige. Even a Mr. Lucas, 'formerly in trade in Meryton', can become a 'Sir William Lucas' of Lucas Lodge, and introduce 'St. James's', the palace where he received his knighthood, into every conversation. 'The distinction [of being knighted] had perhaps been felt too strongly', notes the narrator [of *Pride and Prejudice*] drily. A title, it seems, is sometimes almost a guarantee of fatuousness in Austen's fiction. . . .

Women too sometimes have handles to their names, although they could not inherit a peerage or a baronetcy. Lady Catherine de Bourgh would not want us to miss the fine shades in the title 'Lady'. When it comes attached to the first name—as with Lady Catherine, her sister Lady Anne Darcy, and the unscrupulous Lady Susan Vernon—it signifies that the lady in question has the title 'in her own right', as the daughter of an earl; she is thus 'to the manner [*sic*] born', as the expression goes, and she retains her title irrespective of her husband's status. . . .

Lady Anne Darcy is married to plain Mr. Darcy, and Lady Catherine makes a point of Darcy's family as being 'untitled'. It is nevertheless 'respectable, honorable, and ancient', and Darcy's fortune, at £10,000 a year, is 'splendid'. The long-established but untitled landowning family does seem to gather Austen's deep respect, especially if its income comes from land and a rent-roll; and her two most eligible heroes, Mr. Darcy of Pemberley and Mr. Knightley of Donwell Abbey, come from this class, the landed gentry. . . .

Marriage and Rank

Austen is often happy to follow the Cinderella plot, and to make a happy ending out of marrying her heroine to a man notably above her in income and social prestige. The landowning country gentleman is as close to a prince as her heroines approach. As to income, they usually follow, in effect if not in intention, the prudent advice of [Alfred, Lord] Tennyson's 'Northern Farmer': 'Doänt thou marry for munny, but goä wheer munny is!' Elizabeth's initial rejection of Darcy usefully assures us that she is not marrying him for his £10,000 a year. But she half-jokingly admits that her love has been influenced by 'his beautiful grounds at Pemberley'. Money is only one of a number of factors that count, however.

Elizabeth's marriage to Darcy is the greatest 'match' in the novels, and Mrs. Bennet has every right to rejoice in it. But we have different views on the extent of the social disparity between them. In Lady Catherine's eyes Elizabeth is a nobody, with 'upstart pretensions', a woman shrewdly on the make, who will pollute 'the shades of Pemberley'. Elizabeth herself, however, is not overwhelmed by the social difference. 'He is a gentleman; I am a gentleman's daughter; so far we are equal', she claims calmly. Austen seems to approve of this relative flattening of the degrees of distinction above the country gentry. . . .

The country gentleman, who leads a leisured existence and who subsists on income from land and inheritance, is at his best the moral and social ideal as a partner for a heroine. But the condition takes some living up to: Austen, like other social commentators, insists that with the privileges go extensive responsibilities. Elizabeth freezes Darcy off when he is proud and pretentious; but she warms to him when she discovers how as master of Pemberley he uses his extensive power for the good of those around him. . . .

Rank Within Family

One might suppose that the siblings in a single family would be almost by definition of the same rank. But even here there are marked differences in status, not only between sons and daughters, but also between one son and another. The aristocracy and the inheritance of land depended heavily on the system of primogeniture. Just as only the eldest son can inherit a peerage, so the bulk of land would normally descend by the same systems. The entail, so prominent in *Pride and Prejudice*, legally formalizes this customary practice of inheritance. If an estate were divided equally between all siblings, as our understanding of equitable practice would suggest today, the estate would be dispersed, and would ultimately cease to exist. The system of primogeniture, which unfairly privileges one family member by accumulating all property in his hands, was developed as an arrangement for the preservation of the family name and the family estate through the generations. Austen highlights the injustices of this system of inheritance. . . .

Hence there is a considerable difference in prestige and expectation between elder sons and younger sons, as between sons and daughters. Austen notices this, and dramatizes it; but not without conveying a strong sense of the inequity of such arrangements. The five Bennet girls are to be turned out of Longbourn when their father dies, since the estate is entailed on a distant male cousin, Mr. Collins, who shows precious little sign of being morally worthy of it. Even among these five girls, too, there are notable shades of difference in prestige. Jane, the eldest, is called 'Miss Bennet', while her younger sisters are referred to as 'Miss Eliza', 'Miss Mary', and so on. The elder may be 'out' in society before the younger, and *should* be, according to Lady Catherine; but in this matter, in this family, equity prevails. 'I think it would be very hard upon younger sisters', says Elizabeth, 'that they should not have their share of society and amusement because the elder may not have the means or inclination to marry early.—The last born has as good a right to the pleasures of youth as the first'. Once married, a sister gains prestige over a sister, whatever her place in the age sequence. 'Lord! how I should like to be married before any of you', Lydia tells her elder sisters ingenuously; 'and then I would chaperone you about to all the balls'. And presently—though not without some moral sacrifice—she gains her wish, and takes pride of place at table at her mother's right hand, saying to her eldest sister, 'Ah! Jane, I take your place now, and you must go lower, because I am a married woman'. . . .

The Military Class

A gentleman's son who must earn his living has still rather limited choices in Austen's world: the church, the army, the navy, the law, and medicine (and the last was still of dubious gentility). The army was a doubtful proposition as a living, since an officer's commission had to be purchased. . . .

Austen's preference for the navy over the army is signalled by the notice she takes of their uniforms. The susceptibility of young Kitty and Lydia Bennet to 'the regimentals of an ensign' marks them as 'two of the silliest girls in the country', in their father's opinion; and their foolish mother's wistful fondness for 'a red coat' puts her in the same company. . . .

The Trades and Social Mobility

Austen locates few major characters in 'trade', and for many of her characters the word has a ring that seems to require apology. It is not surprising that the gentry and professional classes felt somewhat threatened by the large changes that were coming with the Industrial Revolution, and tended to close ranks against the newly powerful and the *nouveaux riches*. Trade represents new money, and money, like wine, isn't considered quite respectable until it has aged a little. Austen is clearly fascinated by this process: though she doesn't share the snobbish prejudice against trade, she pays close attention to the gradual assimilation of the trading classes into gentility. . . .

A later stage of this assimilation of one class into another is seen in the Bingleys of *Pride and Prejudice*. Young Charles Bingley is a gentleman of leisure, and already associates with such a prestigious member of the country gentry as Darcy. But his [Bingley's] is new money, 'acquired by trade' in the industrial north of England. We see him in the process of buying his way into the gentry. His father 'had intended to purchase an estate, but did not live to do it'. Bingley, then, in a leisurely manner, is shopping; by renting Netherfield manor, he is trying out country gentlemanhood. Once he marries Jane, he does buy an estate near Derbyshire; so the 'next generation' will be correspondingly a step upward in the social hierarchy. In Bingley we see the best of social mobility. He is good-humoured and charming, and he never stands on ceremony. Like Elizabeth when she moves into Pemberley, he will benefit his new social level by not trying to live up to it all the time. His sisters, however, show the aspect of social mobility that Austen distrusted. They are status-hungry, 'proud and conceited', and Caroline Bingley is over-eager to ally herself and her brother with the prestige of the Darcy family. Conveniently forgetting that her own fortune was made in trade, she is spitefully scornful of Mr. Gardiner, the Bennet sisters' merchant uncle, 'who lives somewhere near Cheapside', she sneers. 'If they had uncles enough to fill *all* Cheapside', Bingley bursts out warmly, 'it would not make them a jot less agreeable'. Generously undiscriminating about shades of social distinction, he cares more about their manners, the amenable social conduct that makes them 'agreeable'. His is the approved attitude.

On this issue, however, Darcy realistically argues that the Bennet sisters' connection with trade 'must very materially lessen their chance of marrying men of any consideration in the world'. His qualification is presented as a point of fact, and he is not malicious, like Miss Bingley. But still, Darcy is to go through an evolution in his attitude, at last marrying, like Bingley, one of the Bennet girls, Cheapside uncle notwithstanding. Indeed, he comes to value the Gardiners, despite their connection with trade, more highly than his father-in-law the country gentleman. The quality of humanity is to be judged by moral and humane standards, Austen suggests, not by social status; but like her own temporary snobs, Darcy and Emma, she pays full attention to their social status first. . . .

Class and the Novelist

It sometimes seems that if class difference did not exist, the novelist would have to invent it, because of the rich potential it provides for definition and fine distinction. Austen, as we have seen, goes in for fine distinctions, whether between the degrees of quality of mind in her characters or the fine shades of difference in their social standing. But to say so much is not to contend that she approved of the bastions of privilege in her very hierarchical society, or resisted the changes towards freer movement between the classes that she saw happening around her. . . .

In Jane Austen's world, human worth is to be judged by standards better and more enduring than social status; but social status is always relevant. With amused detachment, she registers exactly the social provenance of each of her characters, and judges them for the ways in which they judge each other. The importance assigned to class distinction is the source of much of her comedy and her irony, as of her social satire. . . .

'Tinker, tailor, soldier, sailor', goes the rhyme, as the child divines possibilities from the cherry-stones left on the plate; 'Rich man, poor man, beggar-man, thief'. The folk imagination, like the individual's, necessarily busies itself with such matters. Austen's heroines play the cherry-stone game too, and we learn to care whether they will come to reside in 'Big house, little house, pig-stye, barn', and dress in 'Silk, satin, cotton, [or] rags'. Her novels are rich in detail of the status symbols and cultural markers of her society: the estates, lands, houses, cottages; the coaches, carriages, barouche-landaus, hatchments, lozenges, liveries; the silks, satins, muslins, pearls, amber crosses, rings, and beads. As a sensitive and informed commentator on class, that huge topic of the nineteenth century, Austen shows us amply how such things matter. She also shows us how they should not matter too much.

Male Power and Female Talk

Deborah Kaplan

Deborah Kaplan, an associate professor and chair of the English department at George Mason University in Fairfax, Virginia, is the author of Jane Austen Among Women *(1992).*

Deborah Kaplan explores the divide between genders in the patriarchal world of Elizabeth Bennet and the counterculture of women's friendships. The patriarchy, tied to economic conditions and social rank, comes into play during courtship and marriage because only fathers and prospective husbands control the money. Kaplan argues that Elizabeth shows little respect for the rank above her, and she is jealous of the power and independence that aristocratic men, especially Darcy, enjoy, as opposed to the lack of equality and fairness suffered by genteel women, who are little more than pawns in the game of courtship. According to Kaplan, friendships among women in this patriarchy were "the linchpin in Austen's women's culture." Elizabeth's mainstay is her sister Jane, to whom she can talk more freely than she can talk to men.

In her playfully domineering role, Elizabeth refuses the silence and subordination marked out for women; she also assigns desires and sentiments to Darcy, preempting the expression of whatever his own may be. When he asks, "Do not you feel a great inclination, Miss Bennet, to seize such an opportunity of dancing a reel?" she sketches for him a melodramatic scene of an arrogant Darcy victimizing a bravely defensive Elizabeth: "You wanted me, I know, to say 'Yes,' that you might have the pleasure of despising my taste; but I always delight in overthrowing those kind of schemes, and cheating a person of their premeditated contempt. I have therefore made up my mind to tell you, that I do not want to dance a reel at all—and now despise me if you dare."

Challenging Class Patriarchy

In playfully switching roles with Mr. Darcy and assuming his dominance, Elizabeth implicitly challenges his power. In other interactions, with Colonel Fitzwilliam as well as Mr. Darcy, she is explicitly critical. She objects to his willfulness, to the "great pleasure" he takes "in the power of choice." As she tells Colonel Fitzwilliam, "I do not know any body who seems more to enjoy the power of doing what he likes than Mr. Darcy." Everyone, as the Colonel replies, likes to have his or her own way, but Elizabeth, and Colonel Fitzwilliam to some degree as well, are aware of the fact that some are more able to exercise their wills than others. Elizabeth knows that being a man in itself creates opportunities for "the power of choice" that women do not have, and in response to this inequality her recourse is, again, talk.

She watches Mr. Darcy demonstrate power based specifically on gender at a neighborhood ball. Because only gentlemen are endowed with the power to ask women to dance, as only they are empowered to propose marriage, Elizabeth has no option but to wait, partnerless, while Mr. Darcy relishes his power to decide to dance or not. "He walked here, and he walked there," says Mrs. Bennet of his behavior at the ball, and while she is not in general a reliable witness, she captures nicely Mr. Darcy's tendency at the ball to flaunt his power to choose by exhibiting himself detached and free. Single women like Elizabeth, who are not dancing, by contrast remain seated. Elizabeth suffers the embarrassment of his rejection but then challenges his power with verbal mockery, transforming the incident into a story which she tells "with great spirit among her friends."

Gender Within the Class Structure

In or out of marriage, as Elizabeth notes, willful gentlemen like Mr. Darcy have particular advantages due to gender, and again she articulates and criticizes these advantages explicitly. The wife of such a man is very much "at his disposal," she informs Colonel Fitzwilliam. "I wonder he does not marry, to secure a lasting convenience of that kind. But, perhaps his sister does as well for the present, and, as she is under his sole care, he may do what he likes with her."

Gender and Social Independence

Gentlemen also have some opportunities for the exercise of their wills due not specifically to their gender but to the social and economic independence that more generally falls to them because of it. Elizabeth articulates this advantage, broadening her critique to men other than Mr. Darcy. If everyone likes to have his own way, as Colonel Fitzwilliam tells Elizabeth, Darcy does have "better means of having it than many others, because he is rich, and many others are poor." He wishes to contrast himself to Darcy: "I speak feelingly. A younger son, you know, must be inured to self-denial and dependence." But Elizabeth, accustomed to the greater and much more widespread dependence of gentlewomen, refuses to sympathize or to remain politely silent: "In my opinion, the younger son of an Earl can know very little of either. Now, seriously, what have you ever known of self-denial and dependence? When have you been prevented by want of money from going wherever you chose, or procuring any thing you had a fancy for?" She expresses similar irritation at the freedom of choice possessed by Mr. Bingley because of his wealth: "If he means to be but little at Netherfield, it would be better for the neighbourhood that he should give up the place entirely," she insists to Mr. Darcy. "But perhaps Mr. Bingley did not take the house so much for the convenience of the neighbourhood as for his own, and we must expect him to keep or quit it on the same principle."

Bothered by men's social and economic advantages over women, she is quick to identify with Mr. Wickham, the least prosperous and independent gentleman of her acquaintance. In so doing, she reveals the social limits of her sense of injustice: her concern does not extend to women or men beneath the status of the gentry. Mr. Wickham rapidly elicits Elizabeth's sympathy because, as he represents it, his position is similar to that of a marginally *genteel* woman. His father began life, as he tells the heroine, as a country attorney just like her mother's father and her uncle, Mr. Phillips. Promised a clerical living by the elder Mr. Darcy, he finds himself, after the deaths of both his own father and the elder Mr. Darcy, dependent on the heir who, so he claims, has without cause elected not to honor his father's promise. . . .

To convey awareness of sexual inequality and subtle and overt expressions of its unfairness, then, the heroine speaks with a female voice. But again it is important to note that that voice has, in effect, a limited register. If Elizabeth's sympathies do not extend to those without genteel social status, neither in her view does Mr. Darcy's oppression. She is preoccupied with his power only over those with whom she socializes. Not until she visits Pemberley does Elizabeth begin to realize the wide social range on which Mr. Darcy may impose his will: "As a brother, a landlord, a master, she considered how many people's happiness were in his guardianship!—How much of pleasure or pain it was in his power to bestow!" But she comes to appreciate the extensive reach of his power just at the moment when Mr. Darcy's housekeeper persuades her of his benevolent use of it among social inferiors. . . .

Second Culture of Female Friendship

Nevertheless, we cannot determine the moral and political valence Austen assigns to female relationships in *Pride and Prejudice* simply by showing that close female friendships appear in the novel. Our knowledge of Austen's affiliations with two cul-

A scene from the 2007 motion picture "Becoming Jane," directed by Julian Jarrold and starring Anne Hathaway. In the patriarchal world of Jane Austen, courtship was a game in which the women were merely pawns. © Photos 12/Alamy.

tures enables us to see the limitations of this position. Female friendships, to be sure, were the linchpin in Austen's women's culture: they both generated and were represented by that culture. But the gentry's domestic ideology also constructed a version of female friendship. To determine, then, whether female ties in *Pride and Prejudice* express the perspective of the patriarchal culture of Austen's wider community or of the alternative culture of her female friends, we need to explore their functions. . . .

Although *Pride and Prejudice*, then, does offer a series of female friendships, we may construe those alliances as a sisterhood of women only if we mean by sisterhood the affection and support that women give other women. The novel does not portray sisterhood as a political constituency, showing women aware of themselves as a distinct, egalitarian group united in the context of their discontent with patriarchal and hierarchical social relations. *Pride and Prejudice*'s sisterhood is neither antithetical nor alternative to marriage. Elizabeth may be critical of men's privileges and power, but sisterhood does not generate this critique. . . .

That framework will make it possible for us to probe the ending of *Pride and Prejudice* as well. The resolution depicts the heterosexual and hierarchical union that constituted, so the gentry believed, the destiny of feminine women. But does the novel consistently, uniformly endorse that destiny?

The answer, as with commentary on the novel's heroine, depends on the social and literary views of the critics responding. Austen's contemporaries assumed that the plot resolution unilaterally affirmed patriarchal values because they themselves subscribed to those values. . . .

Disguising Social Subordination

Feminist critics, who have commented on the novel's close in recent years, have expressed a much less cheerful view of the marital resolution. Often reminding readers that the nineteenth-century institution of marriage enforced women's legal, economic, and social subordination, they have reperceived Elizabeth and Mr. Darcy's union as a deflating, even degrading fate for the heroine. They disagree, however, over Austen's attitude toward the marriage. Assuming Austen's commitment to it, Mary Poovey, for example, laments that the ending of *Pride and Prejudice* and Austen's other novels serves to "disguise the inescapable system of economic and political domination." "Romantic love," she explains, "seems to promise to women in particular an emotional intensity that ideally, compensates for all the practical opportunities they are denied." . . .

Analyzing the Resolution

A close look at the comic resolution does reveal some subtle, self-conscious divergences from the conventions of comic endings. It is not a glamorous or melodramatic coincidence but the ordinary gossip of Mr. Darcy's aunt that unites the hero with the heroine. Hearing that her nephew and Elizabeth Bennet are on the verge of matrimony, Lady Catherine visits

Elizabeth in order to make her refute this gossip. But in carrying back to her nephew an account of Elizabeth's refusal to deny the report, Lady Catherine unwittingly makes her own gossip the catalyst for Mr. Darcy's second and successful proposal. . . .

[I]t is followed by Elizabeth's concerns about the vulgarity of the treatment that Mr. Darcy receives from her neighbor Sir William Lucas and from her mother, Mr. Collins, and Mrs. Phillips. As the narrator suggests, "though the uncomfortable feelings arising from all this took from the season of courtship much of its pleasure, it added to the hope of the future; and she looked forward with delight to the time when they should be removed from society so little pleasing to either, to all the comfort and elegance of their family party at Pemberley." The narrator also provides a synopsis of their postdenouement married life in which the "pleasures" of Pemberley are frequently interrupted. The insincere Miss Bingley and the condescending Lady Catherine make visits. Lydia repeatedly sends requests for money and comes to stay when her husband goes off to London or Bath. Mr. Bennet, too, though beloved, keeps showing up unexpectedly at Pemberley. . . .

In addition to endorsing marriage as a patriarchal institution, *Pride and Prejudice*'s plot resolution confirms that Elizabeth Bennet's "impertinence," rather than being part of a collective response to a social situation, is unique to her personality. Because it is unique, the heroine's feisty talk has made her lovable. This point is articulated toward the close of the novel when Elizabeth explains to Mr. Darcy why he fell in love with her. . . .

> ". . . You [Darcy] were disgusted with the women who were always speaking and looking, and thinking for *your* approbation alone. I roused, and interested you, because I was so unlike *them*."

Defying Social Restrictions

Emily Auerbach

*Emily Auerbach, professor of English at the University of Wis-
consin–Madison, is the author of* Maestros, Dilettantes, and
Philistines: The Musician in the Victorian Novel *(1989).*

*In the following essay Emily Auerbach suggests that the changes
in expected behavior in* Pride and Prejudice *reveal a gradual
breaking down of social restrictions. Both Elizabeth and her
younger sister Lydia often ignore the proper behavior expected of
a young lady of the gentry or pseudo-gentry. Lydia is vulgar and
irresponsible, and Elizabeth is too lively, independent, and disrespectful. Auerbach contends that many readers of the day believed that Jane, the proper sister, should have been the heroine.
However, it is Elizabeth who is not fooled by the falsities, ignorance, and snobbery of the aristocracy as, for example, when she
bravely counters the rude comments of Lady Catherine, Darcy's
aunt. There are also expectations of "gentlemen." Wickham, Mr.
Collins, Mr. Bennet, and, sometimes, Darcy display only the su-
perficial appearances without the heart of true gentlemen. Ironically, it is the shunned tradesman, Mr. Gardiner, who consistently exhibits the attributes of a true gentleman. The marriage
of Darcy to Elizabeth is a radical event in which the walls between middle-class gentry and aristocracy are broken down.*

Throughout *Pride and Prejudice* Elizabeth [Bennet] jumps,
springs, rejoices, smiles, and laughs, causing conventional
young women to gasp in horror. Miss Bingley and Mrs. Hurst
find her shockingly unladylike. Mrs. Bennet admits that even
though Elizabeth is twenty, she has maintained her girlhood
right to scamper, ramble, and "run on in a wild manner."

Proper Behavior for One's Class

Austen's portrayal of Elizabeth with muddy petticoats and a face glowing with exertion defies the vision of a young woman portrayed in conduct books of the time. Elizabeth Bennet seems not to have read [British author] Hannah More's *Essays on Various Subjects, Principally Designed for Young Ladies*: "That bold, independent, enterprising spirit, which is so much admired in boys, should not, when it happens to discover itself in the other sex, be encouraged, but suppressed."

Elizabeth Bennet also ignores Hannah More's advice that "Girls should be taught to give up opinions betimes, and not pertinaciously carry on a dispute, even if they should know themselves in the right. . . . They should acquire a submissive temper and a forbearing spirit." Rather than submitting, Elizabeth faces adversity with pertinacity and courage. When she arrives at Lady Catherine's formidable mansion, "Elizabeth's courage did not fail her" and she enters "without trepidation." As Elizabeth puts it, "There is a stubbornness about me that never can bear to be frightened at the will of others. My courage always rises with every attempt to intimidate me." . . .

Lydia's Unladylike Actions

What are we to think of Lydia's fearlessness? Like Elizabeth, Lydia is undaunted by authority or convention. Lydia has a "sort of natural self-consequence" and is "self-willed" with a "disdain of all restraint" and an "ungovernable" temper. She is "absolutely resolved" to stay with Wickham, married or unmarried, because it pleases her to do so. Both Elizabeth and Lydia give their opinions decidedly for such young women and display a rebelliousness, irreverence, and audacity. We may admire Elizabeth for asserting herself against the dictatorial Lady Catherine, but what do we think when Lydia cavalierly disregards duty, honor, and gratitude in order to seek her own instant happiness? . . .

The Proper Daughters

Austen frequently sets the "two elder sisters" [Jane and Elizabeth Bennet] apart from the rest of Meryton. When the regiment of officers leaves town, only Elizabeth and Jane respond sensibly: "All the young ladies in the neighbourhood were drooping apace. The dejection was almost universal. The elder Miss Bennets alone were still able to eat, drink, and sleep." They are without question Mrs. Bennet's "two most deserving daughters," both possessing, intelligence, compassion, virtue, and fortitude. . . .

We cannot help but find Elizabeth more compelling, and we already know that the witty Mr. Bennet prefers her. Elizabeth is droll, self-deprecating, perceptive, and loving. And, as Austen expressed it in a letter, Elizabeth is more delightful than previous heroines, different from anything that "ever appeared in print." We may have encountered sweet, angelic, beautiful, modest Jane Bennets before in literature, but no one like Elizabeth. It is not surprising that Elizabeth troubled some in Austen's era, who felt Jane was the novel's true heroine. Author Mary Russell Mitford, for instance, deplored Elizabeth Bennet for possessing an "entire want of taste" and for being "so pert, so worldly a heroine." . . .

Differing Views on Superiors in Rank

Elizabeth has more "quickness" not only in terms of keenness of perception but also in terms of speed. It takes her one moment, not scores of chapters, to reject Miss Bingley and Mrs. Hurst. She does not share the sweet, steady Jane's cautious approach: "I would wish not to be hasty in censuring any one," Jane calmly states. Elizabeth's prejudice stems primarily from her tendency to jump to conclusions as quickly as she jumps over stiles. In a race, one definitely would bet on Elizabeth: "Away ran the girls . . . Jane, who was not so light, nor so much in the habit of running as Elizabeth, soon lagged behind." Elizabeth has to learn to form her own judgments more slowly and cautiously. "All I can promise you . . . is not to be in a hurry," she eventually tells her aunt.

Jane is calmer than Elizabeth and fights against strong emotions like anger. The phrase "pliancy of temper" suggests the narrator's ambivalence about Jane Bennet. Certainly one would not wish to have a rigid, unyielding, utterly stubborn temper, but Jane's pliancy allows her to be too easily bent, influenced, and manipulated by others. She is constantly described as "sweet" and "mild," adjectives suggesting goodness but also a kind of feminine weakness. We cannot imagine Jane standing up so boldly to Lady Catherine, as Elizabeth does. Instead of pertinaciously fighting her adversaries with wit, Jane pliantly withdraws, stays composed, blames herself, and suffers stoically in silence, for "whatever she felt she was desirous of concealing." . . .

Upper-Class Gentleman

As in *Sense and Sensibility*, Austen suggests in *Pride and Prejudice* that idleness and easy wealth threaten to make men effeminate. If Bingley is too pleasing and pliant, Wickham is downright soft, resembling what Austen knew to be the negative stereotype of a woman: "His appearance was greatly in his favour; he had all the best part of beauty, a fine countenance, a good figure, and very pleasing address," "a captivating softness . . . in manners," "every charm of air and address," "every charm of person and address," "He smiled, looked handsome, and said many pretty things." Like Bingley, Wickham is "a young man of most gentlemanlike appearance" who seems all that is "amiable and pleasing," with an "easy assurance," "easy address," and "good-humoured ease." Austen's repetition of identical phrases for Bingley and Wickham seems designed to draw readers' attention to the similarities—and ultimately the key differences. To a *far* greater extent than Bingley, Wickham has acquired the exterior of a gentleman without ethics. Bingley is a rather weak but good man, whereas Wickham is a downright scoundrel, a man whose "vicious propensities—the want of principle" propel him into "a life of idleness and dissipation."

Appearance and Reality

Austen expands her exploration of the gentleman in *Pride and Prejudice* by introducing a gallery of minor male characters with various degrees of gentlemanliness. Mr. Hurst, for instance, "merely looked the gentleman" but is "an indolent man, who lived only to eat, drink, and play at cards." Colonel Fitzwilliam is "not handsome," but his well-informed mind and manner of conversing make him "most truly the gentleman." The only titled gentleman in *Pride and Prejudice* is Sir William Lucas, a knight with "the complaisance of a courtier" who is little more than a timid, unintelligent man in awe of the nobility. Joining Sir William Lucas in his adulation of the rich and titled is William Collins, a ridiculous "mixture of pride and obsequiousness, self-importance and humility" who utters "pompous nothings" and allows himself to be slavishly ruled by the opinions and decrees of Lady Catherine de Bourgh. Mr. Collins is more than stupid: he is mean-spirited. As a way of punishing Elizabeth for refusing his offer, he takes pleasure in spreading the gossip about Lydia and in gloating in his letters to Mr. Bennet that he has not married into their pitiful family: "Let me advise you then, my dear Sir, to console yourself as much as possible, to throw off your unworthy child from your affection for ever, and leave her to reap the fruits of her own heinous offence." Austen shows this clergyman using biblical language ("reap the fruits") to preach a lack of mercy and forgiveness. This is no gentleman, just as this is no man of God. . . .

A True Gentleman

Mr. Bennet's brother-in-law, Mr. Gardiner, would answer that a gentleman lives to help his family and neighbors, not to laugh at them. Austen describes Mr. Gardiner as "a sensible, gentlemanlike man, greatly superior to his sister [Mrs. Bennet] as well by nature as education," a "well-bred and agreeable" man with "intelligence . . . taste and . . . good manners" who marries an equally well-bred, sensible, and loving woman, functions as a loving husband, father, brother, and uncle, and takes dignified action to help the Bennet family with their Lydia troubles. Although, horror of horrors, he "lived by trade, and within view of his own warehouses," Mr. Gardiner is more gentlemanly in manner and deed than those considered his social betters. In passages throughout *Pride and Prejudice* describing "gentlemanlike" behavior, Austen warns readers not to view handsome, leisured men as gentlemen until their just principles, informed understanding, liberal generosity, and active discharge of duties prove them worthy of the name. . . .

A Radical Marriage

It is easy (to use a Bingley term) to be so charmed by the growing love between Elizabeth and Darcy that we fail to recognize the radical social nature of their marriage—and of the novel as a whole. . . . Elizabeth Bennet secures a man worth ten thousand pounds per year and can offer him little besides an embarrassing assemblage of relatives. Not only that but Darcy has noble, titled ancestors while Elizabeth has the taint (also called "pollution" and "impurities") of relatives in trade and in the law. As Austen economics expert Edward Copeland notes, this is "a Cinderella match of great wealth and comparative poverty, across significant social lines," a union of "dizzying" stakes between "potentially one of the most impoverished" heroines and the wealthiest Austen hero.

There is no denying that Austen turns the class system upside down and inside out in this novel. Why else would she go to such lengths to show that the woman at the top of the social ladder—the aristocratic Lady Catherine de Bourgh—has less breeding than the lowly, totally untitled Mrs. Gardiner, the novel's true "lady"? Mrs. Gardiner is "an amiable, intelligent, elegant woman" who shares with her husband "affection and intelligence," or sensibility and sense.

Aristocracy based on birth gives power to those who may not deserve it, Elizabeth Bennet recognizes, and she refuses to feel afraid of Lady Catherine simply because of her title: "Mere stateliness of money and rank, she thought she could witness without trepidation." Elizabeth feels unafraid of Lady Catherine because she possesses no talents or virtues that justify her title and rank. Elizabeth probably shared the thoughts of Figaro in his daring monologue from *Marriage of Figaro*: "Because you're a great lord, you think you've a great mind as well! Nobility, fortune, rank, power, it makes a man proud. What have you done to deserve all that? You went to the trouble of being born, nothing more." Although Lady Catherine enjoys condescending to her social inferiors and "likes to have the distinction of rank preserved," she occupies a superior position merely through accident of birth, not through any talent or merit of her own. Mr. Collins is sure that Elizabeth will temper her "wit and vivacity" when she comes face to face with the great Lady Catherine ("the silence and respect which her rank will inevitably excite"), but Elizabeth in fact responds by voicing her opinions and registering her lack of awe. She feels herself to be Lady Catherine's equal, despite Lady Catherine's noble line and insistence that Elizabeth is "a young woman of inferior birth, of no importance in the world." In her interchanges with Lady Catherine, Elizabeth's firm insistence on equality marks a glorious instance of civil disobedience. An iconoclast, Elizabeth is "the first creature who had ever dared to trifle" with the formidable Lady Catherine. As if proving [British author] Mary Wollstonecraft's assertion that women can think and reason, Elizabeth uses calm logic in her pointed arguments with the enraged Lady Catherine.

In some ways, Austen presents Lady Catherine as an upper-class version of Mrs. Bennet. Darcy feels "ashamed of his aunt's ill breeding" much as Elizabeth feels mortified by her mother's vulgarity. Both women shamelessly put forward their daughters, lack taste and depth, and oppress others with their interference. Both make ridiculously absurd remarks that show they do not know themselves or their own limitations. When it rains and Jane must therefore stay with the Bingleys, Mrs. Bennet acts "as if the credit of making it rain were all her own." Similarly, Lady Catherine is happy to gather a party around her so she can "determine what weather they were to have on the morrow." Mrs. Bennet claims that nobody suffers the way she does, while Lady Catherine insists, "Nobody can feel the loss of friends more than I do." Why might Austen create these parallels? Perhaps she wishes readers to sense that class and wealth are mere accidents of birth and no guarantees of refinement. Give Mrs. Bennet a title, a showy estate, and a sickly unmarried daughter and she could fill Lady Catherine's elegant shoes admirably.

Mrs. Bennet, however, only has the power to make her own family cringe. Lady Catherine inflicts herself on the entire multitude around her, a sort of heartless cross between Louis XIV and Marie Antoinette sallying forth to the poor in order to "silence their complaints, and to scold them into harmony and plenty." Like contemporary bosses micromanaging every aspect of their employees' lives, Lady Catherine gives authoritative commands about everything from the arrangement of furniture to the proper size of joints of meat. She cannot bear Elizabeth's obstinacy, her refusal to kowtow to authority, her upstart ideas, and her nerve in thinking she could marry into such a noble family. . . .

Class Defiance

As if to underscore the political overtones of this clash, Austen uses terms like *dictatorial, magistrate, power, rights, commands,* and *authoritative* to describe the conflict between the imperial Lady Catherine and her defiant subject, Elizabeth. We hear echoes of Lady Catherine in [British playwright Sir W.S.] Gilbert and [British composer Sir Arthur] Sullivan's absurdly haughty Pooh-Bah, The Lord High Everything Else in *The Mikado*: "I can trace my ancestry back to a protoplasmal primordial atomic globule. Consequently, my family pride is something inconceivable. I can't help it. I was born sneering."

Austen does not simplify her presentation of class by implying that all people in lower classes are worthy. Yes, Elizabeth has the very well-bred Aunt and Uncle Gardiner, more deserving of praise than their upper-class "betters," but she also has Aunt and Uncle Phillips, characterized by their vulgarity and strong smell of port. Whether she turns her eyes on aristocrats or those of the middle class, Austen suggests each case must be judged (not prejudged) on its merits.

Rather than concluding *Pride and Prejudice* with a paragraph describing Darcy and Elizabeth's romantic love for each other, Austen chooses to end with an emphasis on the breakdown in walls between the classes. Formerly, Elizabeth had assumed that a marriage to Darcy would have meant separation from her relatives in trade ("my aunt and uncle would have been lost to me"); the Gardiners, she assumes, would be unable to visit Pemberley because of their lower social status. . . .

Laughter as a Leveler

Darcy's ability to overcome his snobbish sense of superiority in order to accept Elizabeth as his equal and to measure her relatives (and his own) by worth rather than birth marks perhaps the greatest personal evolution any Austen hero undergoes.

Darcy has not finished evolving by the end of the novel, though: he has just *begun* to learn how to be laughed at. Laughter is a leveler, so Elizabeth's teasing will keep Darcy from ever becoming a Lady Catherine de Bourgh who condescends to scowl at those of "inferior" ranks. If a wife can laugh at her husband, she claims a kind of equality and security; a right to judge. She is no doormat or admiring doll that, like many a political candidate's wife, claps and smiles no matter how inane her husband's speech. She has a mind of her own and the courage to give voice to her thoughts, however subversive.

Social Issues
in Literature   CHAPTER 3

| Contemporary
Perspectives on
Class Issues

The Uneven Playing Field

Janny Scott and David Leonhardt

Janny Scott reports for the New York Times, *covering stories on housing for the poor and employment, among other subjects. David Leonhardt has been a reporter on economics and business for the* New York Times *since 2000.*

The authors of the following viewpoint assert that the old stereo-types of the upper classes as being Republican and Episcopalian and the working classes as being Democratic union members have changed, causing some to believe that class distinctions have been rapidly disappearing. However, the authors point out that the upper classes isolate themselves from the poor and middle classes, and class mobility has actually lessened. According to Scott and Leonhardt the old threefold division of class into upper, middle, and working (or lower) classes is no longer an accurate description of class structure.

There was a time when Americans thought they understood class. The upper crust vacationed in Europe and worshiped an Episcopal God. The middle class drove Ford Fairlanes, settled the San Fernando Valley and enlisted as company men. The working class belonged to the A.F.L.-C.I.O., voted Democratic and did not take cruises to the Caribbean.

Today, the country has gone a long way toward an appearance of classlessness. Americans of all sorts are awash in luxuries that would have dazzled their grandparents. Social diversity has erased many of the old markers. It has become harder to read people's status in the clothes they wear, the cars they drive, the votes they cast, the god they worship, the color of their skin. The contours of class have blurred; some say they have disappeared.

Class Still Powerful

But class is still a powerful force in American life. Over the past three decades, it has come to play a greater, not lesser, role in important ways. At a time when education matters more than ever, success in school remains linked tightly to class. At a time when the country is increasingly integrated racially, the rich are isolating themselves more and more. At a time of extraordinary advances in medicine, class differences in health and lifespan are wide and appear to be widening.

And new research on mobility, the movement of families up and down the economic ladder, shows there is far less of it than economists once thought and less than most people believe. In fact, mobility, which once buoyed the working lives of Americans as it rose in the decades after World War II, has lately flattened out or possibly even declined, many researchers say.

Mobility is the promise that lies at the heart of the American dream. It is supposed to take the sting out of the widening gulf between the have-mores and the have-nots. There are poor and rich in the United States, of course, the argument goes; but as long as one can become the other, as long as there is something close to equality of opportunity, the differences between them do not add up to class barriers. . . .

Closing and Opening of Ranks

Even as mobility seems to have stagnated, the ranks of the elite are opening. Today, anyone may have a shot at becoming a United States Supreme Court justice or a C.E.O., and there are more and more self-made billionaires. Only 37 members of last year's Forbes 400, a list of the richest Americans, inherited their wealth, down from almost 200 in the mid-1980's.

So it appears that while it is easier for a few high achievers to scale the summits of wealth, for many others it has become harder to move up from one economic class to another. Americans are arguably more likely than they were 30 years ago to end up in the class into which they were born.

A paradox lies at the heart of this new American meritocracy. Merit has replaced the old system of inherited privilege, in which parents to the manner born handed down the manor to their children. But merit, it turns out, is at least partly class-based. Parents with money, education and connections cultivate in their children the habits that the meritocracy rewards. When their children then succeed, their success is seen as earned. . . .

Shifting Notions of Class

One difficulty in talking about class is that the word means different things to different people. Class is rank, it is tribe, it is culture and taste. It is attitudes and assumptions, a source of identity, a system of exclusion. To some, it is just money. It is an accident of birth that can influence the outcome of a life. Some Americans barely notice it; others feel its weight in powerful ways.

At its most basic, class is one way societies sort themselves out. Even societies built on the idea of eliminating class have had stark differences in rank. Classes are groups of people of similar economic and social position; people who, for that reason, may share political attitudes, lifestyles, consumption patterns, cultural interests and opportunities to get ahead. Put 10 people in a room and a pecking order soon emerges.

When societies were simpler, the class landscape was easier to read. [Karl] Marx divided 19th-century societies into just two classes; Max Weber added a few more. As societies grew increasingly complex, the old classes became more heterogeneous. As some sociologists and marketing consultants see it, the commonly accepted big three—the upper, middle and

Bill Gates, CEO of Microsoft, is part of the new class system in which the richest one percent of Americans make 2 trillion more dollars than the bottom ninety percent of society. AP Images.

working classes—have broken down into dozens of micro-classes, defined by occupations or lifestyles. . . .

Less Mobility Than Expected

The new studies of mobility, which methodically track peoples' earnings over decades, have found far less movement. The economic advantage once believed to last only two or three

127

generations is now believed to last closer to five. Mobility happens, just not as rapidly as was once thought. . . .

One study, by the Federal Reserve Bank of Boston, found that fewer families moved from one quintile, or fifth, of the income ladder to another during the 1980's than during the 1970's and that still fewer moved in the 90's than in the 80's. A study by the Bureau of Labor Statistics also found that mobility declined from the 80's to the 90's. . . .

One surprising finding about mobility is that it is not higher in the United States than in Britain or France. It is lower here than in Canada and some Scandinavian countries but not as low as in developing countries like Brazil, where escape from poverty is so difficult that the lower class is all but frozen in place.

Those comparisons may seem hard to believe. Britain and France had hereditary nobilities; Britain still has a queen. The founding document of the United States proclaims all men to be created equal. The American economy has also grown more quickly than Europe's in recent decades, leaving an impression of boundless opportunity.

But the United States differs from Europe in ways that can gum up the mobility machine. Because income inequality is greater here, there is a wider disparity between what rich and poor parents can invest in their children. Perhaps as a result, a child's economic background is a better predictor of school performance in the United States than in Denmark, the Netherlands or France, one recent study found.

"Being born in the elite in the U.S. gives you a constellation of privileges that very few people in the world have ever experienced," Professor [David I.] Levine [Berkeley economist and mobility researcher] said. "Being born poor in the U.S. gives you disadvantages unlike anything in Western Europe and Japan and Canada." . . .

Collapsing of Stereotypes

The economic changes making material goods cheaper have forced businesses to seek out new opportunities so that they now market to groups they once ignored. Cruise ships, years ago a symbol of the high life, have become the ocean-going equivalent of the Jersey Shore. BMW produces a cheaper model with the same insignia. Martha Stewart sells chenille jacquard drapery and scallop-embossed ceramic dinnerware at Kmart.

"The level of material comfort in this country is numbing," said Paul Bellew, executive director for market and industry analysis at General Motors. "You can make a case that the upper half lives as well as the upper 5 percent did 50 years ago."

Like consumption patterns, class alignments in politics have become jumbled. In the 1950's, professionals were reliably Republican; today they lean Democratic. Meanwhile, skilled labor has gone from being heavily Democratic to almost evenly split.

People in both parties have attributed the shift to the rise of social issues, like gun control and same-sex marriage, which have tilted many working-class voters rightward and upper income voters toward the left. But increasing affluence plays an important role, too. When there is not only a chicken, but an organic, free-range chicken, in every pot, the traditional economic appeal to the working class can sound off key.

Religious affiliation, too, is no longer the reliable class marker it once was. The growing economic power of the South has helped lift evangelical Christians into the middle and upper middle classes, just as earlier generations of Roman Catholics moved up in the mid-20th century. It is no longer necessary to switch one's church membership to Episcopal or Presbyterian as proof that one has arrived.

"You go to Charlotte, N.C., and the Baptists are the establishment," said Mark A. Chaves, a sociologist at the University of Arizona. "To imagine that for reasons of respectability, if you lived in North Carolina, you would want to be a Presbyterian rather than a Baptist doesn't play anymore."

The once tight connection between race and class has weakened, too, as many African-Americans have moved into the middle and upper middle classes. Diversity of all sorts—racial, ethnic and gender—has complicated the class picture. And high rates of immigration and immigrant success stories seem to hammer home the point: The rules of advancement have changed.

The American elite, too, is more diverse than it was. The number of corporate chief executives who went to Ivy League colleges has dropped over the past 15 years. There are many more Catholics, Jews and Mormons in the Senate than there were a generation or two ago. Because of the economic earthquakes of the last few decades, a small but growing number of people have shot to the top.

"Anything that creates turbulence creates the opportunity for people to get rich," said Christopher S. Jencks, a professor of social policy at Harvard. "But that isn't necessarily a big influence on the 99 percent of people who are not entrepreneurs."

These success stories reinforce perceptions of mobility, as does cultural myth-making in the form of television programs like "American Idol" and "The Apprentice." . . .

Class, Education, Health, and Housing

Clearly, a degree from a four-year college makes even more difference than it once did. More people are getting those degrees than did a generation ago, but class still plays a big role in determining who does or does not. At 250 of the most selective colleges in the country, the proportion of students from upper-income families has grown, not shrunk.

Some colleges, worried about the trend, are adopting programs to enroll more lower-income students. One is Amherst [in Massachusetts], whose president, Anthony W. Marx, explained: "If economic mobility continues to shut down, not only will we be losing the talent and leadership we need, but we will face a risk of a society of alienation and unhappiness. Even the most privileged among us will suffer the consequences of people not believing in the American dream."

Class differences in health, too, are widening, recent research shows. Life expectancy has increased over all; but upper-middle-class Americans live longer and in better health than middle-class Americans, who live longer and in better health than those at the bottom.

Class plays an increased role, too, in determining where and with whom affluent Americans live. More than in the past, they tend to live apart from everyone else, cocooned in their exurban [out of the city, past the suburbs] chateaus. Researchers who have studied data from the 1980, 1990 and 2000 censuses say the isolation of the affluent has increased. . . .

Those widening differences have left the educated and affluent in a superior position when it comes to investing in their children. "There is no reason to doubt the old saw that the most important decision you make is choosing your parents," said Professor Levine. . . . "While it's always been important, it's probably a little more important now.". . .

Class in the Future

Will the trends that have reinforced class lines while papering over the distinctions persist?

The economic forces that caused jobs to migrate to low-wage countries are still active. The gaps in pay, education and health have not become a major political issue. The slicing of society's pie is more unequal than it used to be, but most Americans have a bigger piece than they or their parents once did. They appear to accept the tradeoffs. . . .

The idea of fixed class positions, on the other hand, rubs many the wrong way. Americans have never been comfortable with the notion of a pecking order based on anything other than talent and hard work. Class contradicts their assumptions about the American dream, equal opportunity and the reasons for their own successes and even failures. Americans, constitutionally optimistic, are disinclined to see themselves as stuck.

Blind optimism has its pitfalls. If opportunity is taken for granted, as something that will be there no matter what, then the country is less likely to do the hard work to make it happen. But defiant optimism has its strengths. Without confidence in the possibility of moving up, there would almost certainly be fewer success stories.

Marriages That Cross Class Lines

Tamar Lewin

Tamar Lewin, journalist for the New York Times *since 1982, has written stories on education, anti-Semitism, social policy, and gender issues.*

As part of the New York Times *series "Class Matters," the following article examines the "cross- class marriage," a situation that occurs repeatedly in* Pride and Prejudice. *The middle-class Elizabeth Bennet marries the upper-class Darcy, and her sister, Jane, marries a man whose family made a fortune in trade. In this twenty-first century instance explored by Tamar Lewin, a Catholic working-class man without a college education marries a wealthy upper-class Jewish woman. Yet neither religion nor ethnic background creates the need for adjustment; it is their difference in class. Ironically, Lewin describes that it is the husband who is most troubled by the differences in their backgrounds. Generally speaking, this includes differences in education, differences in views about money and how to manage it, and different manners, choices of food, and ideas about child rearing. At the root of their problem is a lifetime of different experiences. As in* Pride and Prejudice, *this couple also has to learn to accept each other's different families.*

When Dan Croteau met Cate Woolner six years ago, he was selling cars at the Keene, N.H., Mitsubishi lot and she was pretending to be a customer, test driving a black Montero while she and her 11-year-old son, Jonah, waited for their car to be serviced.

The test drive lasted an hour and a half. Jonah got to see how the vehicle performed in off-road mud puddles. And Mr. Croteau and Ms. Woolner hit it off so well that she later sent him a note, suggesting that if he was not involved with someone, not a Republican and not an alien life form, maybe they could meet for coffee. Mr. Croteau dithered about the propriety of dating a customer, but when he finally responded, they talked on the phone from 10 p.m. to 5 a.m.

They had a lot in common. Each had two failed marriages and two children. Both love dancing, motorcycles, Bob Dylan, bad puns, liberal politics and National Public Radio.

Problems of Cross-Class Marriage

But when they began dating, they found differences, too. The religious difference—he is Roman Catholic, she is Jewish—posed no problem. The real gap between them, both say, is more subtle: Mr. Croteau comes from the working class, and Ms. Woolner from money.

Mr. Croteau, who will be 50 in June, grew up in Keene, an old mill town in southern New Hampshire. His father was a factory worker whose education ended at the eighth grade; his mother had some factory jobs, too. Mr. Croteau had a difficult childhood and quit school at 16. He then left home, joined the Navy and drifted through a long series of jobs without finding any real calling. He married his pregnant 19-year-old girlfriend and had two daughters, Lael and Maggie, by the time he was 24.

"I was raised in a family where my grandma lived next door, my uncles lived on the next road over, my dad's two brothers lived next to each other, and I pretty much played with my cousins," he said. "The whole concept of life was that you should try to get a good job in the factory. My mother tried to encourage me. She'd say, 'Dan's bright; ask him a question.' But if I'd said I wanted to go to college, it would have been like saying I wanted to grow gills and breathe underwater."

He always felt that the rich people in town, "the ones with their names on the buildings," as he put it, lived in another world.

Ms. Woolner, 54, comes from that other world. The daughter of a doctor and a dancer, she grew up in a comfortable home in Hartsdale, N.Y., with the summer camps, vacations and college education that wealthy Westchester County families can take for granted. She was always uncomfortable with her money; when she came into a modest inheritance at 21, she ignored the monthly bank statements for several years, until she learned to channel her unease into philanthropy benefiting social causes. She was in her mid-30's and married to a psychotherapist when Isaac and Jonah were born.

"My mother's father had a Rolls-Royce and a butler and a second home in Florida," Ms. Woolner said, "and from as far back as I can remember, I was always aware that I had more than other people, and I was uncomfortable about it because it didn't feel fair. When I was little, what I fixated on with my girlfriends was how I had more pajamas than they did. So when I'd go to birthday sleepovers, I'd always take them a pair of pajamas as a present."

Outside the Comfort Zone

Marriages that cross class boundaries may not present as obvious a set of challenges as those that cross the lines of race or nationality. But in a quiet way, people who marry across class lines are also moving outside their comfort zones, into the uncharted territory of partners with a different level of wealth and education, and often, a different set of assumptions about things like manners, food, child-rearing, gift-giving and how to spend vacations. In cross-class marriages, one partner will usually have more money, more options and, almost inevitably, more power in the relationship.

It is not possible to say how many cross-class marriages there are. But to the extent that education serves as a proxy for class, they seem to be declining. Even as more people marry across racial and religious lines, often to partners who match them closely in other respects, fewer are choosing partners with a different level of education. While most of those marriages used to involve men marrying women with less education, studies have found, lately that pattern has flipped, so that by 2000, the majority involved women, like Ms. Woolner, marrying men with less schooling—the combination most likely to end in divorce. . . .

Bias on Both Sides

When he met Ms. Woolner, Mr. Croteau had recently stopped drinking and was looking to change his life. But when she told him, soon after they began dating, that she had money, it did not land as good news.

"I wished she had waited a little," Mr. Croteau said. "When she told me, my first thought was, uh oh, this is a complication. From that moment I had to begin questioning my motivations. You don't want to feel like a gold digger. You have to tell yourself, here's this person that I love, and here's this quality that comes with the package. Cate's very generous, and she thinks a lot about what's fair and works very hard to level things out, but she also has a lot of baggage around that quality. She has all kinds of choices I don't have. And she does the lion's share of the decision-making."

Before introducing Ms. Woolner to his family, Mr. Croteau warned them about her background. "I said, 'Mom, I want you to know Cate and her family are rich,'" he recalled. "And she said, 'Well, don't hold that against her; she's probably very nice anyway.' I thought that was amazing."

There were biases on the other side too. Just last summer, Mr. Croteau said, when they were at Ms. Woolner's mother's house on Martha's Vineyard, his mother-in-law confessed to

Britain's Prince Charles and Princess Diana on their wedding day in 1985. Their highly publicized "cross-class" union contributed to their difficulties in marriage. AP Images.

him that she had initially been embarrassed that he was a car salesman and worried that her daughter was taking him on as a kind of do-good project. . . .

Confusing Differences

Mr. Croteau had [an] experience [at] Northfield Mount Hermon [prep school]. . . . He briefly had a job as its communications manager, but could not adjust to its culture.

"There were all these Ivy Leaguers," he said. "I didn't understand their nuances, and I didn't make a single friend there. In working-class life, people tell you things directly, they're not subtle. At N.M.H., I didn't get how they did things. When a vendor didn't meet the deadline, I called and said, 'Where's the job?' When he said, 'We bumped you, we'll have it next week,' I said, 'What do you mean, next week? We have a deadline, you can't do business like that.' It got back to my supervisor, who came and said, 'We don't yell at vendors.' The idea seemed to be that there weren't deadlines in that world, just guidelines."

Mr. Croteau says he is far more comfortable at the hospital [where he now works as a software analyst]. "I deal mostly with nurses and other computer nerds and they come from the same kind of world I do, so we know how to talk to each other," he said.

But in dealing with Ms. Woolner's family, especially during the annual visits to Martha's Vineyard, Mr. Croteau said, he sometimes finds himself back in class bewilderment, feeling again that he does not get the nuances. "They're incredibly gracious to me, very well bred and very nice," he said, "so much so that it's hard to tell whether it's sincere, whether they really like you." . . .

Inequalities

And there are moments when the inequalities within the family are painfully obvious.

"I do feel the awkwardness of helping Isaac buy a car, when I'm not helping them buy a car," Ms. Woolner said of the daughters. "We've talked about that. But I also have to be aware of overstepping. Their mother's house burned down, which was awful for them and for her and I really wanted to help. I took out my checkbook and I didn't know what was appropriate. In the end I wrote a $1,500 check. Emily Post doesn't deal with these situations."

She and Mr. Croteau remain conscious of the class differences between them, and the ways in which their lives have been shaped by different experiences.

On one visit to New York City, where Ms. Woolner's mother lives in the winter, Ms. Woolner lost her debit card and felt anxious about being disconnected, even briefly, from her money.

For Mr. Croteau, it was a strange moment. "She had real discomfort, even though we were around the corner from her mother, and she had enough money to do anything we were likely to do, assuming she wasn't planning to buy a car or a diamond all of a sudden," he said. "So I didn't understand the problem. I know how to walk around without a safety net. I've done it all my life."

Both he and his wife express pride that their marriage has withstood its particular problems and stresses.

"I think we're always both amazed that we're working it out," Ms. Woolner said.

But almost from the beginning they agreed on an approach to their relationship, a motto now engraved inside their wedding rings: "Press on regardless."

Girls and Classism

Stephanie Jones

*Stephanie Jones, professor of literacy at Teachers College of Co-
lumbia University, is the author, with Rhoda H. Halperin, of
"Academic Borderlands: MICROgirls, a Math Club for Girls," in
Halperin's* Whose School Is It? *(2006).*

*Teacher-author Stephanie Jones follows eight elementary school
girls as they are introduced to the practice of reading literature
critically and relating it to their own poverty-stricken backgrounds. Each girl, and Jones herself, grew up in abject poverty
at the bottom of the social structure in the United States. None
of the girls have knowledge of a larger world outside their trailer
parks and ghettoes; they had no prior knowledge of the upper
economic classes that they encountered for the first time in school.
The following passages are taken from the girls' discussions with
Jones about a book they have read and liked, featuring middle-
class characters. The teacher-author leads the girls to relate the
book to their own lives as a means of defining class and their
positions in society. They also discover through their reading that
other people have family lives, clothes, and possessions different
from their own.*

One version of Lori's [a mother of a student] philosophy
of education . . . focused on gaining students' interest by
starting with their lives. The following quote extends her
thinking but it turns our attention to the "perfect lives" of
book characters that Lori believed many children encountered
each day in their language arts education:

> Because [kids in St. Francis] see things all the time—and
> they read these little stories in school about all these perfect

lives, and mommy and daddy work and blah—*that* is not how it is. You have a mom who gets a check once a month whose daddy's on the street corner selling *drugs* whose kid is—you know—sittin' there with people comin' in and out of the house who *buy* drugs and they see this, yet they're goin' to school learnin' about perfect little Jill's life and this and that—and that's *bull*crap because that's not how it is.

Reality and Fiction

Lori chose a hypothetical "Jill" to represent all that is disconnected from the lives of children in St. Francis within the books they often read in classrooms, and she intuitively understood that constant interaction with these mainstream stories was not healthy for children who lived very different lives. In an ironic twist, Lori's daughter Cadence was the reader who I first noticed making up "fictions" about her life to seem more like a character that was living a seemingly perfect life— Henry was his name. Like Lori's reference to a "Jill," "Henry" will be used in this chapter, but the Henry I refer to is the main character in a series of books written for early readers that Herbert Kohl would describe as "middle class in character, [that ties] well-being to money and portray[s] lives full of comfort and joy." The Henry I refer to here is the beloved pre-adolescent White, middle-class boy from the *Henry and Mudge* series written by Cynthia Rylant.

This chapter will begin by reconsidering the "basics" of reading instruction to include a critical perspective in the reading workshop and exploring what I call the Multicultural Trap of critical literacy. Then I will describe a series of events in the second grade classroom around *Henry and Mudge* and my attempt to add one simple tool for challenging the books' representations of a normal life. And finally, this chapter will end with work that I did with the girls as they were entering fifth grade when we critically analyzed *Henry and Mudge* through "Disconnections" between their lives and the books.

These disconnections led to insightful conversations around assumptions and stereotypes based on social class. . . .

Ignoring Class Realities

I fell victim to this multicultural trap as a second-grade teacher; my students were exposed to literature with characters and situations that did not reflect mainstream America. We discussed perspectives, critically considered social issues, asked ourselves about the use of power, and explored how the books made us feel and what they made us think. Our critical literacy "work" with written text was often focused around progressive sophisticated children's literature that was read aloud by me given the challenging text and the students' emerging practices as code breakers. However, I never deconstructed a mainstream text in front of the students, and I never gave them the tools they needed to do it themselves as they read independently in Reading Workshop. When they were faced with books that seemed to present "normal" lives in a mainstream way, the growing readers in the classroom worked hard as code breakers, text participants, and text users. But they were certainly not text analysts. One example was in their reading of *Henry and Mudge*. . . .

Challenging the Literacy Picture

The following transcript is from one of the videotaped small group meetings around *Henry and Mudge* books. Beginning with general questions about the books within the series, I eventually moved toward scaffolding students' critical reading of the text by asking, "What would you change about this story to make it more like your life?" Once I began questioning the text, its representation of "family," and asking the students what they might change, the discussion moved toward text analysis and the critical reading of oneself into a story.

STEPHANIE: So you have told me all the things you like about these stories, what if you could change something about them—what would you change?

SARAH: Like the names of the characters and the characters.

STEPHANIE: Who would you change?

SARAH: The dog or the father.

ANNIE: First change the father.

STEPHANIE: Okay, change the father or the dog. Into—what do you mean?

SARAH: Change him into a scientist (giggles from all three girls).

STEPHANIE: Okay, he could be a scientist. Or maybe he wouldn't have to be there at all, right? You could take the father out of the book altogether?

I inserted this possibility because Sarah's father was in jail at the time and she seemed under pressure to suggest an alternative "father" that would fit within the mainstream discourse of the *Henry and Mudge* series (a white-collar professional father) rather than suggest something that might reflect her world.

SARAH: And add the father as a big brother or somethin'.

Sarah had several older male cousins and uncles that were important in her life, but no older brothers. However, she suggested an alternative to the family structure in the text that she understood intimately.

STEPHANIE: Ohhh. So maybe there could be a big brother instead of a father? I'm wondering if you started writing a new series like this, hmmm. I'm wondering where you could say the father went. Why wasn't the father there?

SARAH: We could say he's at work.

ALEXIS: Or he's lazy.

Sarah and Alexis were speaking within competing discourses around fathers, or men in general, in the community of St. Francis. Sarah suggesting that fathers do, in fact, work, and Alexis suggesting that if they don't work, they are lazy. A more critical reading of not working, however, would recognize the lack of work available to many of the adult men in St. Francis who had not completed high school and relied heavily upon their manual labor and market demands for such things as painting, drywall installation, and so on.

STEPHANIE: Okay, he could be lazy or he could be at work.

ANNIE: Or he could be in jail.

STEPHANIE: He could be in jail.

SARAH: He could be in a car.

STEPHANIE: Okay, so if you each started thinking about . . . hmmm. I love to read *Henry and Mudge* stories too, I think they're great stories—but, when I look at this family it doesn't really look like my family. I don't know if it looks like Alexis' family.

Following this prompt, the girls' enthusiasm increased as well as their use of gestures and they began moving around on the floor. Considering a change in one character was fine, specific. But opening up the possibility that the entire family structure can be called into question seemed to excite them.

ALEXIS: No, I have *mass* more people.

STEPHANIE: How 'bout you Annie? Does this look like your family?

ANNIE: No (shakes head no and opens eyes wide).

STEPHANIE: How 'bout you, Sarah?

SARAH: No.

STEPHANIE: So maybe Cynthia Rylant wrote about a family she knew, but if we started to write stories like this we'd have to change it a lot, wouldn't we? To write about things that we really know.

SARAH: It looks like my aunt's 'cuz they live in a house and um, they gots a backyard with a dog in it and stuff.

STEPHANIE: Really? So this looks like your aunt's family?

SARAH: Yeah, my aunt _____, she lives in Florida.

Sarah had discussed her aunt before, noting that she lives in a neighborhood with "big houses" and near "doctors and lawyers." . . .

The girls were listening intently but admittedly had never really considered how books did *not* connect with their life experiences. I asked them to give it a try as they flipped through the pages of *Henry and Mudge* books looking at the illustrations. . . .

Class Stereotypes

Studying the same illustration of Henry, his mother, father, uncle, and cousin sitting at a long dining room table, Cadence piqued the group's interest in the girl cousin who was wearing a bow in her curly hair and a frilly white dress.

"She's like different. She acts like she's different from the rest of the family," Cadence pointed out.

"She don't eat all that stuff," suggested Heather.

"What do you mean?" I asked.

"She eats like lobster," Heather told us.

"Oh, you think she eats lobster?" I asked.

"Yeah, she looks like a little rich girl," Heather sneered.

"Oh, she looks like a little rich girl, what do you mean by that?" I probed.

Heather responded by describing her white frilly dress, her hair bow, and Cadence joined in. Sarah, however, sat quietly.

"Do you think she looks like a rich girl?" I asked Sarah. She responded by shaking her head no quietly. "Tell us about that."

"'Cuz, I ain't rich, but I ain't poor, but I got dresses," she tells us matter-of-factly.

"She looks like a little spoiled brat. Look at her purse," added Heather, "this is how she walks, I'm serious," she told us as she stood up to perform what she considered a spoiled brat walk. Again, Heather is reading the illustration to understand not only material lives, but also the social practices of the characters.

"I never look like *that* until like Easter or Christmas," Cadence told the group.

"She just looks like she's not used to—she looks like she's from a fancier place," stated Sarah.

"To eat lobster!" yelled Heather, glad that Sarah is finally seeing her point.

"And eat out," added Cadence.

The girls continued to look through the books when Heather found the evidence she had hoped for, "Oh my God! She *is* spoiled, that's her *room*! Look at her teacups and her hankies."

"Do you have a disconnect, Heather?" I asked her.

"Yeah, I ain't got all that stuff on my wall."

Sarah jumped in, "Heather, but you're spoiled too."

"No I'm not!"

"Yes you are!"

"There's her bed. She is spoiled," Heather pointed to a canopy bed in the cousin's spacious bedroom.

"I have a canopy too, but mine ain't just like that. But I got the circle," Sarah told us.

The conversation continued and began to incorporate money when Cadence stated that she was not like that girl (in the book) at all, because she didn't get everything she wanted and she had to do chores around the house to even get any money from her mom. The other girls had a different experience with money, however, and Sarah told us that she was given $40.00 each week by her father to have fun with and pay her cellular phone bill. This was a great opportunity for me to challenge the girls, again, to consider multiple perspectives and to resist stereotyping or essentializing people the way that they had been essentialized by people for so long.

"You have a *phone*?" I asked, surprised.

"I do too," said Heather.

"I been having a phone since I was eight," Sarah added.

"Now some people, Sarah, might say that only really rich kids have phones," I stated.

"Nu-huh," said Heather.

"Oh, that is *not* true!" Sarah shouted in disbelief.

"Why?" I asked.

"'Cuz," Sarah shrugged.

"We're not really rich and we both have a phone," Heather told me.

"My cousin, her mom used to be real bad on drugs and then she got better, she's been better for a couple months, and they got 'em an apartment and stuff, and she ain't got a job yet, but my cousin gots a phone, and her brother gots a PlayStation 2 and stuff like that, and they ain't rich," Sarah told the group.

I pulled out a notebook and pen, "So there are lots of in-betweens. So it you have rich over here (I draw a line on a piece of notebook paper)—and you have really poor over here (another line is drawn on the opposite side of the paper). There's lots of stuff in the middle, right?"

"And you're doing okay, like," added Heather.

"Like not so rich and not so poor," Cadence finished.

After this acknowledgement of the gray areas between the extremes of rich and poor, the girls began talking about people who "act" rich, or "goody-goody" even when they are not. The conversation shifts from material possessions and money to the *performance* of social class—something that makes thinking about such issues even more complex.

I began to probe them about the goody-goody concept, "And you said 'goody-goody.' Does that mean that you have to be rich to act goody-goody?"

"No," Sarah stated slowly with her eyebrows raised.

"Confusing isn't it?" I asked the girls.

"Like goody-goody, is like when you're not really rich, but you're really perfect and you just act like you're rich and act like you got everything but you don't," Sarah explained.

"Like, you said this cousin [in the *Henry and Mudge* book] looks goody-goody," I said.

"Yeah," said Sarah.

"Because if somebody is like . . ." Cadence began.

"She has *teacups* on her wall!" shouted Heather.

"What does that mean though?" I asked.

"She's rich!" Heather yelled.

"She could be spoiled, but her family could, probably couldn't be rich, they probably just like her to," Sarah began.

"Do stuff," Heather added, again focusing on the performance of social class.

"People don't have to be rich and there's uhhh, ugh!" Cadence was starting to get quite frustrated. It had all seemed so simple before this discussion.

I laughed a little and Heather mimics what she perceived as a performance of a rich girl, "People be like," she continued in a high-pitched sing-songy voice, batting her eyelashes and exaggerating the pronunciation of each word, "'Mommy, can I have the money to get a dress?' Just like on the Fresh Prince of Bel Air," Heather brought in her knowledge of girl performances in a wealthy household from a television show.

Throughout this conversation that began with a frilly-dressed girl in a simple illustration, the girls began to articulate their local understandings of social class difference and the roles that material goods, money, and performance play in social class. Beginning with assumptions and stereotypes, the girls were able to work through when and why some were simply wrong and that a perspective that takes into account individual people and practices and relativity might be more productive than the rich-poor dichotomy and how people are perceived and judged based on where they might be considered within the spectrum.

Single Women and Happiness

Sarah Mahoney

Sarah Mahoney, a writer living in Maine, has contributed several articles to AARP The Magazine.

Jane Austen and her sister, Cassandra, never married. In their day, society considered unmarried women failures and placed them in the lowest rank among adult family members. This attitude persisted into the nineteenth and twentieth centuries in the United States, but according to Sarah Mahoney, stereotypes of unmarried women—notions that they are invariably sad, stubborn, resentful, and lonely—have proved inaccurate. Almost half of the 57 million American women who are forty-five or older are single; AARP polled 2,500 of them to learn their views of their lives. The poll found that rather than being lonely, many of these single women are very contented with their lives. In another AARP poll, some of the single women (ages forty through sixty-nine) date, but about 10 percent have no interest in dating. Many value their independence more than having lasting relationships. Mahoney concludes that research is mixed on the health of single women as opposed to married ones, but the single woman is no longer stigmatized as she was in Austen's day.

It is often said that females are complex and mysterious creatures, hard to understand and completely unpredictable. But older single women seem to have a mythology all their own. They are lonely, they long for love, they are terribly afraid of dying destitute. When Bella DePaulo, Ph.D., a psychology professor at the University of California, Santa Barbara, and author of the forthcoming book *Singled Out*, asked 950 college students to describe married people, they used

Sarah Mahoney, "The Secret Lives of Single Women," *AARP The Magazine*, May 2006. Reproduced by permission of the author.

words like "happy, loving, secure, stable, and kind." The descriptions of singles, on the other hand, included "lonely, shy, unhappy, insecure, inflexible, and stubborn."

Are the stereotypes true? Is the picture that bleak? Or are these women in fact loving their independence and having the time of their lives? What really goes on behind the closed doors of the millions of single women in America? To find out, AARP recently polled more than 2,500 women ages 45 and older for its landmark AARP Foundation Women's Leadership Circle Study. Though this group is large and diverse, the results, presented on the following pages, may surprise you.

The Number of Single Women

Mind you, these are not rare birds: of the 57 million American women 45 and up, nearly half—25 million—are unmarried (outnumbering entire populations of countries such as North Korea, Taiwan, and Australia). There are several reasons for this: American women marry later, their divorce rate is high, and, not to put too fine a point on it, those who are married are likely to outlive their mates. As a result, American women are now likely to spend more years of their lives single than with a significant other, according to DePaulo. Instead of having some single stretches in between relationships, she says, "the reality is relationships are now what happens between longer periods of singleness." . . .

Against Stereotype

Whatever their type, it's clear that words like *lonely*, *shy*, and *insecure* no longer apply. Fully half the women in our study say they are happier than they've ever been. Are they sad now and then? Sure—aren't we all? Do they occasionally lose sleep worrying about the future? Yes, and with good reason: being a single older woman comes with its own economic challenges. But that doesn't stop the majority from believing that midlife offers an opportunity for growth, for learning, and the chance to do the things they've always wanted to do. In fact, says De-Paulo, "many single women are living lives of secret content-ment." Now, let's take a closer look at the facts and fiction about single older women in the United States today. . . .

Is a Relationship Essential?

Given the option, many single women wouldn't mind a com-mitted relationship with a cuddly, caring partner—preferably someone with minimal emotional baggage and the kind of in-come to support a nice summer house, facts supported by an AARP survey, "Lifestyles, Dating & Romance: A Study of Midlife Singles." It finds that 31 percent of single women 40 through 69 are in an exclusive relationship, and another 32 percent are dating nonexclusively. But it also finds that a sur-prising number couldn't care less. About one in 10 have no desire to date at all, and another 14 percent say that while they'd date the right guy if he came along, they aren't going to knock themselves out trying to find him. (The remaining 13 percent are, indeed, looking.)

In fact, most of those who aren't dating seem disinclined to change that situation anytime soon. Among 40-plus women who hadn't been on a date in the past three years, 68 percent say they just aren't interested in dating or being in a romantic relationship, though 61 percent of them would reconsider if they met someone interesting. Those who do date say it re-quires a philosophical balance between putting on a game face on Saturday night and not getting stressed if nothing devel-ops. "I'm dating, and I'd like to find a good relationship," says Flo Taylor, 54, a TV producer in Pittsburgh. "But if it doesn't happen for me, I'm fine with that, too." . . .

Inevitably Lonely?

Living alone can be lonely. AARP's "Sexuality at Midlife and Beyond" survey found that 28 percent of single women said that within the past two weeks they had felt lonely occasionally or most of the time, compared with only 13 percent of married women in the same category. Slightly more single women (93 percent) than their married sisters (87 percent), however, said they felt their independence was important to their quality of life. "I love the freedom, and the fact that I know so many other single women I can network with," says Flo.

The key, says Brenda Bufalino, 68, a dancer and choreographer who lives in New York City, is to accept that some days will be lonely—no matter who you are. "The other day my granddaughter asked me, 'Nana, don't you ever get lonely?'" Bufalino, who's been divorced since 1973, answered her, "Sure, but I got lonely sometimes when I was married, too." . . .

Concern About the Future

The majority of single women (81 percent) aren't overly concerned about the prospect of growing old alone, according to the AARP Foundation women's study. Among those who do worry, divorced women (25 percent) fret more than widows (19 percent) and married women (17 percent). And in fact some single women recognize that their single status will actually protect them from the heartbreaking (and often health-breaking) ordeal of caring for a sick husband in his declining years.

For older women, married or single, life can prove challenging whether they fret about it or not. "Married women may enter their 60s better off than women who are single, divorced, or widowed," says Cindy Hounsell, executive director of the Women's Institute for a Secure Retirement. "But through divorce or death, they lose their husbands and many financial benefits of being married. By age 85 the majority are single. That's the astonishing thing—most of us are going to be single."

The truth is that with no spouse to help care for them, women are more likely than men to wind up in nursing

Actress Kristin Davis is one of many famous and successful single women who have helped change the once popular notion that single women are invariably lonely and sad, and true happiness and success lies only in marriage. AP Images.

homes. And they are also more likely to get chronic illnesses than men are, says Heidi Hartmann, Ph.D., a labor economist and president of the Institute for Women's Policy Research. If the abstract fear of winding up alone doesn't worry single women, the concrete threat of becoming dependent on caregivers does. According to the AARP Foundation women's study, some 41 percent of women who live alone worry that they might lose their independence in a health crisis, versus 35 percent of women who live with a spouse or other adults. A related fear, shared equally by married and single women alike, is imposing on their children at some point in the future. About 31 percent of women who live alone, and 30 percent of women who live with others, say they are at least moderately worried about eventually becoming a burden to their family. . . .

Single Women Have Good Lives

For decades health researchers have consistently found that married women are healthier than single women. But the most negative health outcomes for women have been associated with those who are divorced or widowed. Very little attention has been paid to the long-term health outcomes of women who are contentedly single. One surprising finding to come out of the AARP Foundation women's survey, however, is that single women tend to think of themselves as healthy—46 percent said their health is excellent or very good. In addition, 90 percent of the single women in the study said they're very or somewhat confident that they're doing all they can to keep themselves healthy. "These findings seem promising," says Jean Kalata, AARP research analyst and principal researcher for the AARP Foundation women's study, "but we need more research into single women and the effects of happiness on health."

So, is being single the new happy ending for American women? Of course not. But it doesn't mean life is over. As more unmarried women embrace the challenges and opportunities that come with living alone, they are writing new chapters in self-discovery, says Florence Falk, Ph.D., a psychotherapist in New York City and author of *On My Own: The Art of Being a Woman Alone*, due out in January 2007. "Many women are surprised at how learning to be alone, in the best sense of the word, opens them up to a bigger world. Even with the speed bumps, being single can lead them to better relation-ships, more creativity, new friendships, and a deeper sense of self and community."

The Widening Gap

Chris Spannos

Chris Spannos, previously a social service worker in Vancouver, is a writer and an antiwar organizer.

Chris Spannos believes that the class war of the twenty-first century is being waged by the elite against all the rest of society; it is not so much a war between classes. His evidence for this is the concentration of immense wealth in the hands of 300,000 Americans and the growing gap between rich and poor. After years of industrial progress, the United States is facing economic disaster.

Analysts and pundits alike all have common understanding of the following words for explaining and remedying the current state of the U.S. economy: "recession," "inflation," "housing crisis," "economic stimulus package," "rate cuts," and "injections." However it doesn't take an economist, a Wall Street banker, nor a college graduate to understand these could also be euphemisms summarizing what has been happening: Class War in the opening of the 21st Century. Except the war is not yet a war between classes, it is a war waged by elites on the rest of us. And the war is not new.

The Growing Class Divide

Many already know of the widening wealth gap in the U.S.; 2005 saw the largest growth in share of national income for the top 1 percent of Americans since 1928. During 2005 "the top 300,000 Americans collectively enjoyed almost as much income as the bottom 150 million Americans." Corresponding with these figures the top 10 percent reached a level of income share not seen since before the Great Depression. With that in

Chris Spannos, "Consciousness for Classlessness: A Necessity for the Class War," *Znet*, January 25, 2008. Reproduced by permission of the author.

mind, it seems less a coincidence to hear that the current crisis is [according to Robert Kuttner] the "most serious financial crisis since the Great Depression, and we've only begun to see how bad it is?" We are experiencing an upward redistribution of wealth unprecedented in the last 100 years while at the same time facing an economic disaster. It would take a Wall Street banker to not see how these dots connect.

[Stanly Aronowitz notes,] "This is not a narrow working class interest. We're losing, essentially, a century of industrial and economic progress. Even as we speak. And that is a good way to form a class alliance.". . .

A Goal of Classlessness

Our Class is defined by material and social groupings with others who have the same interests, needs, and self-conceptions within the economic sphere of society. Strategizing against the war being waged on us by elites should be for improved working and living conditions—yes. But ultimately, the goal that usually escapes discussion, is Classlessness. . . .

Evidence of Class Change

But great strides in historical change for the better are not unprecedented. In 2008, of two leading presidential candidates in the U.S. one is a woman, and another African American. Ending Jim Crow racism was real. Winning universal suffrage was real. However, the people who made that history possible struggled against the belief that those oppressive social and material relations were either the product of divine inheritance or historical outcome. Shedding light on the possibility of attaining a classless and participatory society, and that this is no different than ending elite power and privilege based on race or gender, is key for demythologizing its needed realization. . . .

Do the Elite Deserve Their Positions?

Reproduction of class within capitalism, from the perspective of those at the top, requires the self-aggrandizing fallacy, that they somehow deserve their ownership of productive assets, high salaries and wages, and managerial authority. The fallacy "rationalizes" how they worked hard, or simply come from better "stock," and that their wealth, power, and privilege are their just desserts.

Most people stay in the class they are born into and their economic fates are pre-determined. In The State of Working America 2006/2007, while looking at intergenerational class mobility, its authors ask "To what extent are children's economic fates tied to their parents' income or wealth? Do most families end up about where they started on the income scale?" and "Is the United States' less-regulated economy characterized by greater economic mobility?" The authors' research finds that income, wealth, and opportunity are "significantly" correlated across generations. A daughter of a low-income mother has only a small chance of achieving very high earnings in her adulthood. "Almost two-thirds of children of low wealth parents (those in the bottom 20 percent of wealth scale) will themselves have wealth levels that place them in the bottom 40 percent of the scale." Their research also shows that the U.S. has become "considerably" less mobile over time, and has even less class mobility than other advanced economies. . . .

The Working Class

Realizing a classless society should be as fundamentally important as attaining a society free from racism, sexism, and authoritarianism. Yet abolishing wage labor, markets, and corporate hierarchies, along with racism and sexism, remains our unfinished project [as stated by Russian anarchist Mikhail Bakunin]:

"Slavery may change its form or its name—its essence remains the same. Its essence may be expressed in these words:

to be slave is to be forced to work for someone else, just as the master is to live on someone else's work. In antiquity . . . slaves were, in all honesty, called slaves. In the Middle Ages, they took the name of serfs; nowadays they are called wage earners." . . .

The Classes of Workers, Managers, and Owners

"From political economy itself, using its own words, we have shown that the worker sinks to the level of a commodity, and moreover the most wretched commodity of all; that the misery of the worker is in inverse proportion to the power and volume of his production; that the necessary consequence of competition is the accumulation of capital in a few hands and hence the restoration of monopoly in a more terrible form; and that, finally, the distinction between capitalist and land-lord, between agricultural worker and industrial worker, disappears and the whole of society must split into the two classes of property owners and propertyless workers."

A scathing observation of the capitalist system, but, this two-class analysis doesn't go far enough. This is where Bakunin's brilliance shines through. Bakunin saw a third class between "the two classes of property owners and propertyless workers" and he predicted the "Red Bureaucracy" which rose within the Russian Revolution, which also came to plague the predominant examples of "Actually Existing Socialism" in the 20th Century. Bakunin specifically called into question the conceptual oxymoron of "dictatorship of the proletariat," while also exposing the false higher value of conceptual labor over manual labor underlying the self-aggrandizing beliefs of the coordinator class:

"Do not the manager's superior training and greater responsibilities entitle him to more pay and privileges than manual workers? Is not administrative work just as necessary to production as in manual labor—if not more so? Of course,

The immense concentration of wealth in the hands of a select few contribute to the widening gap between the rich and the poor. © Paul Maguire/Alamy.

production would be badly crippled, if not altogether suspended, without efficient and intelligent management. But from the stand point of elementary justice and even efficiency, the management of production need not be exclusively monopolized by one or several individuals. And the managers are not at all entitled to more pay. . . . The monopoly of administration, far from promoting the efficiency of production, on the contrary only enhances the power and privileges of the owners and their managers." . . .

The orthodox two-class analysis is concerned mostly with class struggle as the driving force shaping society and history. . . .

Challenging the class war being waged by elites is informed by holding a three-class analysis highlighting, not only the gap between rich and poor, but relations between workers, coordinators, and capitalists. In seeking class alliances we can strategize to see which coordinators workers can ally themselves with, we can see which coordinators will side with the capitalist against workers, and we can adjust our strategies today accordingly for a new approach which embodies our hopes for classlessness tomorrow.

For Further Discussion

1. How did class divisions affect Jane Austen's life? (See Kelly, Lauber, and Butler.)

2. After a thorough study of the novel, discuss and write about Jane Austen's view of the eighteenth-century class system as it comes through in the novel. Does she accept and endorse it or does she disapprove of it? Does she seek to change the system? (See Spring, Keymer, Monaghan, McAleer, and Auerbach.)

3. Discuss in some detail the place of money in social interaction, social mobility, and courtship. (See Monaghan and Copeland.)

4. Note the place of courtship in the novel. How does it operate in reference to class in *Pride and Prejudice* and today? (See Kent, McMaster, Lewin, Jones, and Mahoney. Also contribute your own ideas.)

5. What role do gender limitations play in the class system of Elizabeth Bennet's world? (See McMaster and Kaplan.)

6. Compare and contrast class divisions in *Pride and Prejudice* and today. Bring your own experience to your discussion. (See Keymer, Scott and Leonhardt, and Spannos.)

7. Examine the effect that the French Revolution and the Industrial Revolution had on the Bennets' lives. (See Kent and Eagleton.)

For Further Reading

Jane Austen, *Emma*, 1815.

Jane Austen, *Mansfield Park*, 1814.

Jane Austen, *Northanger Abbey*, 1817.

Jane Austen, *Persuasion*, 1817.

Jane Austen, *Sense and Sensibility*, 1811.

Charlotte Brontë, *Jane Eyre*, 1847.

Emily Brontë, *Wuthering Heights*, 1847.

Charles Dickens, *Great Expectations*, 1861.

F. Scott Fitzgerald, *The Great Gatsby*, 1925.

Samuel Richardson, *Clarissa*, 1747–1748.

Samuel Richardson, *Pamela*, 1740.

Bibliography

Books

Juliet Prewitt Brown
Jane Austen's Novels: Social Change and Literary Form. Cambridge: Harvard University Press, 1979.

Alistair M. Duckworth
The Improvement of the Estate: A Study of Jane Austen's Novels. Baltimore, MD: Johns Hopkins University Press, 1971.

Mary Evans
Jane Austen and the State. London and New York: Tavistock, 1987.

John Halperin, ed.
Jane Austen: Bicentenary Essays. Cambridge, England: Cambridge University Press, 1975.

Richard Handler and Daniel Alan Segal
Jane Austen and the Fiction of Culture: An Essay on the Narration of Social Realities. Tucson: University of Arizona Press, 1990.

Manwai C. Ku, Szonja Szelenyi, and David B. Grusky, eds.
Social Stratification: Class, Race, and Gender in Sociological Perspective. Boulder, CO: Westview Press, 2008.

Rhoda F. Levine, ed.
Social Class and Stratification: Classic Statements and Theoretical Debates. Lanham, MD: Rowman and Littlefield, 2006.

David Monaghan
Jane Austen: Structure and Social Vision. London: Macmillan, 1980.

Jane Nardin	*Those Elegant Decorums: The Concept of Propriety in Jane Austen's Novels.* Albany: State University of New York Press, 1973.
New York Times	*Class Matters.* With an introduction by Bill Keller. New York: Times Books, 2005.
Michael Zweig	*What's Class Got to Do with It?: American Society in the Twenty-first Century.* Ithaca, NY: Cornell University Press, 2004.

Periodicals

Dan Andrews and Andrew Leigh	"More Inequality, Less Social Mobility." *Social Science Research Network* (September 2007).
Joan Austen-Leigh	"Forms of Address and Titles in Jane Austen." *Persuasions: Journal of the Jane Austen Society of North America.* 12 (December 1990): 35–37.
Felicia Bonaparte	"Conjecturing Possibilities: Reading and Misreading Texts in Jane Austen's *Pride and Prejudice.*" *Studies in the Novel* 37, no. 2 (Summer 2005): 141–161.
David Brooks	"The Sticky Ladder." *New York Times* (January 25, 2005).
K. St. John Damstra	"The Case Against Charlotte Lucas." *Women's Writing* no. 2 (2000): 165–174.

D.G. Greene — "Jane Austen and the Peerage." *PMLA* 68 (1953): 1017–:31.

Susan C. Greenfield — "The Absent-Minded Heroine: Or, Elizabeth Bennet Has a Thought." *Eighteenth-Century Studies* 39, no. 3 (Spring 2006): 337–350.

Sandra MacPherson — "Rent to Own; Or What's Entailed in *Pride and Prejudice*." *Representations* 82 (Spring 2003): 1–23.

Edward Neill — "'Found Wanting'? Second Impressions of a Famous First Sentence." *Persuasions: Journal of the Jane Austen Society of North America* 25, (2003): 76–84.

Jacqueline Reid-Walsh — "Mistress of All She Surveys: Elizabeth Bennet Claims Pemberley as Her Own." *Female Spectator* 8 (2003): 16–19.

Judith Terry — "Seen but Not Heard: Servants in Jane Austen's England." *Persuasions: Journal of the Jane Austen Society of North America* 10 (1988): 104–116.

Index

S

Satire
    of aristocracy, 16
    by Austen, 68, 88
    gentry class, 23
    social class distinction, 22, 105
Scott, Janny, 124–132
Scott, Walter, 96–97
Sense and Sensibility (Austen), 26, 28, 38, 79, 116
Sense of superiority, Darcy, 36, 104, 121
Sentimental comedy, 35–36
Sentimentalism, rural gentry, 19
Sexuality at Midlife and Beyond (AARP survey), 152–153
Single women, 150–156
Singled Out (DePaulo), 150–151
Sisterhood, social relations, 110
Smith, Adam, 76
Snobs/rascals
    aristocracy as, 11, 21, 57, 59, 113
    Darcy as, 63, 121
    social status of, 37–38, 104
Social class, Elizabeth *vs.* Darcy
    and Bingley, 61, 63–64
    courtship, dancing, 59–60
    identity *vs.* individualism, 72
    patriarchy, challenges to, 107, 110, 110*f*
    prejudice, by Darcy, 59–61
    prejudice, by Elizabeth, 57–59
    rudeness, 58, 61–63
    stereotyping, 58, 64, 145–149
Social class, structure
    classlessness appearance, 124
    commoners, 51
    economy of, 34, 52, 126, 140
    education in, 125, 130–131
    in England, 52

future concerns, 131–132
gender issues, 108
independence within, 50
language, 43–44
life expectancy, 131
nobility, 9, 11, 52, 59
political parties, 129
power, 125
religion, 129–130, 134–135
shifting notions, 126–127
stereotypes, collapsing, 129–130
Social class, value changes
    courtship between, 9–10, 33
    defiance over, 120–121
    gentry, responsibility, 91–92
    manners, importance, 70, 93–95, 104
    mobility, 92–93
    political upheaval, 87–88
    self-parody, Austen, 88–89
    titles *vs.* love, 95–96
Social class, widening, 157–160
Social criticism, 21–22, 40, 68, 92
Social distinctions, and morality
    class mobility, 67–69
    crisis over, 90
    disinheritance, 65
    genteel class, 89
    lack of, 71–73
    soldier class, 66–67
    training, 89–90
    well-being, 59
Social distinctions, between classes
    the aristocracy, 53–54
    battles between, 84–85
    of the Bennets', 45–47
    in bourgeois, 45–46
    between gender, 25, 109
    hybrid, 47
    lack of, 43
    military officers, 83